MYTH, HISTORY AND FAITH

MYTH, HISTORY AND FAITH

The Remythologizing of Christianity

by

Morton T. Kelsey

PAULIST PRESS
New York / Paramus / Toronto

Library of Congress
Catalog Card Number: 73-94216

ISBN: 0-8091-1827-0

Published by Paulist Press
Editorial Office: 1865 Broadway, N.Y., N.Y. 10023
Business Office: 400 Sette Drive, Paramus, N.J. 07652

Printed and bound in the
United States of America

ACKNOWLEDGMENTS

The Collected Works of C. G. Jung, ed. by G. Adler, M. Fordham, H.
Read, and W. McGuire, trans. by R. F. C. Hull, Bollingen Series XX, vol.
10, *Civilization in Transition* (copyright © 1964 by Bollingen Foundation) ; vol. 11, *Psychology and Religion: West and East* (copyright © 1958
by Bollingen Foundation and © 1969 by Princeton University Press) ; vol.
12, *Psychology and Alchemy* (copyright 1953 by Bollingen Foundation and
© 1968 by Princeton University Press. Reprinted by permission of Princeton University Press and Routledge & Kegan Paul, London.

Myths After Lincoln by Lloyd Lewis. New York: Harcourt Brace Jovano-
vich, Inc. Used with permission of the publisher.

Memories, Dreams, Reflections by C. G. Jung. Recorded and edited by
Aniela Jaffe and translated by Richard and Clara Winston. New York:
Pantheon Books, A Division of Random House, Inc. Used with permission.

Saturday Review, December 7, 1963. New York: Saturday Review/World,
Inc. Reprinted by permission.

Los Angeles Times, February 28, 1964, letter of Mrs. Annalee Whitmore
Fadiman. Used with Mrs. Fadiman's permission.

The Day Lincoln Was Shot by Jim Bishop. Copyright © 1955 by Jim
Bishop. Reprinted by permission of Harper & Row, Publishers, Inc.

Contents

I Your *Man* Is Too Small 1

II Myth in History 14

III Myth and the Problem of Evil 35

IV The Dying and Rising God 56

V Jesus of Nazareth 71

VI Some Misconceptions about Myth 88

VII Psychology, Philosophy and Myth 106

VIII Religion and Myth 122

IX Sharing in the Victory: The Practice of Prayer. . 145

X Myth and Sacrament 169

Notes 181

To my grandchildren
Chris and Katie
that they may know
the vitality and power
of the Christian story

I
Your *Man*
Is Too Small

There is real confusion and anxiety among Christians today about the future of religion. Among intellectuals in the church there is growing concern that men do not need religion any more. Now that man has "come of age," he seems to get along very adequately with only his reason, his sense experience, and the science which he thinks comes solely from them. He no longer seems to need the myths and symbols of the Christian faith. And so Christian thinkers have suggested that these are outmoded, primitive ways of thinking which are no longer useful now that man has become mature in the ways of the secular world.[1]

At the same time there is every indication of a crisis of faith. The current statistics show that churches and seminaries, religious orders and philanthropies, both Catholic and Protestant, are affected. Nor is the trouble confined just to lay people; it is widespread among the clergy themselves.[2] Theological formulations and popular religious practices which stood for centuries have crumbled away in the last twenty years. Vatican II opened a great spring, as in a rocky mountainside, but most people have not learned what to do with so much fresh, living water. They often seem to be drowning in it rather than channeling it to refresh the arid land.

The great tragedy in this is that there is no real need

for the confusion. The crisis exists, but not because it was inevitable or necessary. Instead, it is a result of man's failure to use the full range of his capacities. Man in this Western world of ours has been trained to concentrate on such a limited portion of reality that he has been brainwashed almost as successfully as if he lived under a Communist or Fascist regime. He has forgotten the depth and complexity of his own psyche (or soul or personality, call it what you wish), and the kind of knowledge that can touch it. He believes that everything he knows comes to him consciously, as a product of his reason and his senses, which tell him that he is one tiny outgrowth of an obviously physical universe. Man finds himself a speck on a limitless plain of energy and matter, none of which speaks with any certainty about God or any other religious reality. The fact that this idea of the world seems so obvious, however, should alert us to ask some questions. It is very often the obvious things, those we accept at face value without reading the fine print, that need to be examined the most carefully.

In reality, our view of man is too small. We know there are people whose God is too small, but we seldom see that there is a connection between small man and small God, or that one idea often leads to the other. Yet God has ways of communicating, and the human being has all sorts of depths and capacities for responding, which have been ignored. In the beginning the scientists were trying, carefully and with good reason, to discover the regularities in the world around us, and they decided to consider only those capacities of man which they needed to use at that time. Probably their decision was a necessary one, in order to lay the foundations of science.

Gradually, however, these other human abilities were pushed aside and forgotten. Even the church, much of it, came to disregard man's capacity to think in images and stories, in sagas and legends, in symbols and myths. We need to realize once more that these are the tools men use to tell about their contact with another realm of reality, a spiritual one. As we shall see, there is no good reason to doubt either the existence of such a level of reality or man's capacity to be touched by it. He finds it in his religious experiences, in his dreams, his visions and intuitions and ecstasies, in religious healings and prophetic guidance, and all the ways that were once described in religious writings, and in the myths of most religions.

It is not indecent to discuss these things, in spite of the opinion of many thinkers in the church. Many of them have bowed to the secular world by agreeing that man does not have this kind of capacity. They have then tried to shape their ideas about religion in purely secular or intellectual terms. This has not been very fruitful, since myth is integral to almost every one of man's religions, and particularly to Christianity. Myth is essentially the way man talks about his religious encounter with God and the spiritual world.* Eliminate it, and man doesn't have much to talk about religiously; his religion becomes meaningless and flat, or else compulsive.

Myth and Truth

At this point we need to take a good look at the meaning of this very important word "myth," which is apparently hard to understand today. Many people, in both religious and secular circles, have accepted a popular usage of the word which suggests that myths are simply stories that are not true. According to this view, the myth is either an outright falsehood or a product of fanciful imagination with no relation at all to real life. It may

---

*The reader who finds that he needs a logical approach to the understanding of myth should read Chapters VI and VII and then return to the present discussion.

be produced consciously, or it may arise spontaneously from the depth of the unconscious, but either way it has nothing to do with the hard, material realities of the world around us. One can hold to this view of myth, however, only by forgetting the depths and capacities of the human psyche and insisting that man is strictly matter, or physical being, and nothing more. One must also ignore the way myth has been understood in other times, by peoples fully as intelligent and wise as we of the scientific era.

It is this older, more complete understanding of myth to which many perceptive students of mythology are returning. These men, some of them renowned scientists in their own fields, have realized that mythological images refer to a part of reality which cannot be described in ordinary language. Myths, according to these students, are as necessary as the language we use to describe objects and experiences in the outer world. The difference is simply that they speak of another realm of reality and experience, other than the physical one.

Myth in this sense is understood as a story or series of images describing man's contact with the world of spiritual realities which interact with the physical world and give it form. Man's life is the main stage (although not the only one) on which spirit and matter touch each other. Because this contact can only be described mythologically, man's myths are usually relevant to the physical world as well as to the spiritual realm. Myth and truth are not opposed to one another. Nor is myth contrary to the factual record of history; instead each gives an account of the facts from its own point of view, history looking at them from the outer physical side, myth from the inner spiritual side.

Undoubtedly there are certain myths that were created consciously by men to fill the gaps in their understanding of nature, or to set up and give authority to a particular social or religious group. But these are "inventions" rather than *myths* in the sense we are describing, and they represent only a portion of this kind of story. There are many true *myths* which describe man's contact with realities other than those of the physical world. These stories rise out of the depths of the unconscious. They speak of the meaning and significance of spiritual reality, and how it interpenetrates and affects the familiar physical world. They cannot be called concoctions to explain something in nature that is not yet understood; they are not fanciful, pre-scientific thinking. On the contrary this kind of myth is one important way that man shares his knowledge and experience of the world of spirit that touches him even while he lives in the midst of the physical world.

The early church did not often use the word myth to describe the Christian message, because this word was usually applied to the pagan deities and their activities. But it was never used to suggest that those gods were not real, but only that they were partial and therefore evil. The Christians of earlier times believed in a world of spirit such as we are describing, and they used stories and myths freely to tell of man's contact with it. They just did not call it by that name.

Naturally if one does not believe in any such level of reality, then myth becomes something of a puzzle, or even a hindrance to man's effort to get on with the business of clean, sensible, rational, materialistic living. On the other hand, some of the most creative and forward looking scientists have come to the conclusion that scientific discovery itself is not possible without thinking in images and symbols and myths. This has given myth and imagination a new place in men's thinking.

Lacking any use of myth, man becomes only a partial human being, because he has lost his principal means of dealing with spiritual reality. What I am suggesting is that there are realities of spirit which determine the forms of the physical world around us. And even more, these same realities or patterns form the warp of human life, and can be touched by man directly in his deepest experiences. Much of the time these patterns of spiritual reality are quietly at work without the help of man's conscious mind. But now and again they can break through in an individual life, giving that life a powerful direction for good or evil. These patterns of reality have far more meaning, however, than just as primeval instincts or urges. In fact these things—spiritual beings if you wish to call them that—frequently show a higher development than our human personalities. But trying to catch their drift without knowing their language or how to deal with them is like going fishing without any hooks.

There are heights and depths to man and the world around him that twentieth century men have overlooked, and it is these reaches that may be experienced and expressed in myths which can give meaning and direction to our lostness and confusion. In this sense there is no opposition between myth and history. Along with being dreamed or imagined or intuited, myth can also be seen weaving itself into the fabric of history. Any of the pictures or stories that describe these spiritual realities, these patterns of meaning, may be expressed in the events of history. In the next chapter we shall consider how the myth of "the dying god," which is found among nearly all peoples, was played out in the events surrounding the assassinations of two American presidents. This myth is still very much alive in people of our own day. But only as people see what is happening do they have some means of directing their destiny. Let us see what has occurred as men have tried to ignore myth.

Man without Myth

There was a time when men could live serenely within their villages or valleys, ignoring the rest of the world unless it came invading. But today the world itself has shrunk into a tight little ball. Events that disrupt one part can affect lives everywhere. Morning after morning one may be greeted on the Today Show by turmoil in Africa or the Middle East, and in his morning paper by violence and murder in our own country. The death of a president, the terror in Munich, political machinations in Chicago or Washington or Saigon, student uprisings in almost every country, all have an effect on us. And these things are like mere echoes of the endless wars we have fought since 1914.

At the same time men have lost any sure conviction that their lives have meaning. They doubt that there is anything beyond the physical world. At this very time when men most need meaning and direction to turn to, they find in most places the attitude that only skill and science and reason count. If there is any meaning to be found they must go back to the turmoil and look for it.

This understanding was put into final form by the thinkers of the nineteenth century. But with the advent of universal education, the attitude which had been the property of only a few intellectuals suddenly belonged to everyone. It stated out and out that man's religious beliefs and even his philosophies, for the most part, were childish ways of looking at the world. Man had come of age, it held, and needed only the solid information and understanding provided by science. There could be no use for myths or religious traditions. Stories about heaven and hell, man's soul, the afterlife, God, or angels were merely inventions to help man get by in a world without science. Why would he go back to such fanciful explanations of things when the real experiences of science were surely and safely making his world a better place to live in?

It is not difficult to trace the beginnings of this attitude. In the sixteenth century the whole world view of the Middle Ages collapsed when Copernicus showed that the earth moved around the sun and that man was not the center of the universe. He could no longer believe that hell was right under his feet in the bowels of the earth or that earth was surrounded by ten circles of practically physical heaven inhabited by the saints, angels and God himself. Until that time no one had really questioned the medieval understanding, which Dante described so magnificently in the *Divine Comedy*. This view was far from naive, and it had helped man through one of the most difficult periods of history. But with Copernicus it was gone and there was nothing to take its place, and no one had offered a view that would help men relate to the universe they were beginning to discover.

Instead, a revolution was beginning. In the following century Newton discovered the laws of motion and applied them to the planets, as well as to things like bullets and falling rocks. As chemistry followed along, applying these principles to the rest of matter, man found himself up against a universe of inert substances and mathematical laws. All the changes in matter, even in flesh and bone and brain cells, could be explained like a game played with 92 billiard-ball atoms, according to the rules of Newton's physics. With Darwin's understanding that human development is entirely due to natural selection through survival of the fittest, the system of naturalism was complete. Man could explain anything from the smallest atom to the farthest star; he could even explain himsef in purely physical terms, with no need to consider how a world of spirit might influence the physical one.

At this point men began to ask some very significant questions. Where in a world like this is the place for God? Does he have any effect on this world? What about morality, heaven and hell, and man's soul? And on another level, what about the miracles of the Bible and stories like the crossing of the Red Sea and the resurrection? What does one do with the angels and demons, dreams and visions and stories of healing which touch half the verses of the New Testament? If the scientific thinking of 1900 was right, then these things are fabrications and they are called "myth" in the sense of an untrue story, told by less intelligent men either to explain something they did not understand, or to make some difficulty they were unable to cope with more bearable. To this way of thinking, the comforting myths of the New Testament have no meaning for a modern scientific society. It was more polite and respectful to call them myth than plain lies or falsehoods.

One after another the Christian thinkers adopted this thesis. They began to suggest that mature men must live with the world just as science finds it. The authentic modern man must realize that myths are interesting, but of no use for the twentieth century. They should be cut out of his life and from his Bible. Only those parts of the Bible that are free of myth—its morality and history— should be taken seriously. And this is just where many theologians are today. They deny that Christians came by their religion in any of the ways described in the New Testament, and they are scrambling around trying to fit God and Biblical religion into this picture of the world.

With this kind of doubt and confusion among religious thinkers, men are forced to search for meaning on their own. They face fear and anxiety; they have to deal with aggression and hostility which cause misery within and between men. They suffer an almost indefinable heaviness, and they often live with depression day in and out which most psychiatry seems powerless to heal. Or again, they express the lostness outwardly in alcoholism and drug addiction. It appears that none of these disturbances can be healed except by a sense of meaning, given by a contact with that reality from which meaning originates.*

In trying to understand themselves and their place in the world, however, people take some of the strangest and most diverse routes. Popular psychology floods the book stalls: *I'm OK, You're OK* has been a best seller for over a year, and *Walden II*, B. F. Skinner's story of a materialistic utopia, has sold over a million copies. People pay incredible prices for psychological help, and still the demand exceeds the supply. There are not enough trained helpers to go around.

Various publications offer popular guidance on dream interpretation, like the recent article for teen-agers in *Seventeen* and a special tear-out "dream-book" featured in *Cosmopolitan*. Some people are even attracted to witches' covens and Satan cults. And then there are still others who seek in specifically religious ways, through Pentecostal experiences, or in the Jesus Movement, or by making pilgrimages to follow the 15-year-old Hindu leader Maharaj Ji.

Countless others look for direction even farther afield, turning to Transcendental Meditation, or delving into the ancient arts of astrology and divination by dreams, or by more occult methods like Tarot cards or palmistry. Reams of material pour out on astrology, and the daily horoscope in the newspaper is as much a ritual for many people as morning coffee. When religion fails to meet these strange experiences with its wisdom for handling them, men are on their own, to flounder or muddle through.

At the same time, the churches that are trying to live without myth, the orthodox, middle-of-the-road churches that try to follow what is left of the Christian message, are dwindling and afraid for the future. Could it be that

---

*I have discussed this psychological problem in more detail in a paper on the subject of "Intervening with Meaning." It is one that needs a lot of attention and thought.

the intellectuals were wrong? That something is missing from their picture of a world of stark material reality? That even that world still has need of myth and things of spirit?

A Way Out

Strangely enough, just as people were trying to get used to that kind of world, science began to see it differently. Physics and chemistry, mathematics and anthropology, medicine and psychology, each in its own way, began to question the materialistic certainty of nineteenth century science. This change, which we shall describe in a later chapter, has opened up a way for the use of myth once again. And how grateful people are when they are unhooked from their demythologized world and are given techniques for dealing with spiritual reality through images and myths.

In twenty-five years of parish work, and almost as long lecturing to both clergy and lay people in this country and abroad, I have seen the importance of myth for people's lives. As men and women come to see that myth is not opposed to either history or science, but reveals something which ordinary science cannot touch, many of those who have lost meaning turn back again to the reality of the Christian message. In my parish, with the able help of Dr. Ollie Backus, we found that large numbers of people, both sophisticated and more simple, were able to recapture the reality of Christian faith as they were helped to approach myth and reality in this way. Far from making them less appreciative of science, or less effective in the outer world, the experience of myth in their own lives released them to be more so.

For the last four years I have been working with graduate and undergraduate students at Notre Dame. Among them are some of the brightest and most sincere men and women I have known, who were struggling to find meaning in life. Many of them were at sea, with no way to hold on to their traditional faith. They had been immersed in the ideas of nineteenth century science, or in the existential writers who capitulated to it, and there seemed to be no answers in the rational theology they had been taught as young people. As they began to understand the inadequacy of these views, and realized how open-minded the most recent scientists are, they found that the world of myth could be considered again.

They discovered that there is a reality within and behind the myth which could touch them, and that the Christian message had real meaning for them. They understood why Robert Oppenheimer, almost twenty years ago, had begged the assembled American Psychological Association not to base their psychological understanding on the model of "a physics which is not there any more," an outdated model of certainty in a material system.[3] These students, preparing themselves for today's world, were relieved to discover that convictions about a world of meaning alongside the physical one were not nearly as questionable as they had believed. Their religion took on a new importance.

Through a great many experiences like these I have come to know that myth speaks of a reality, a realm which cannot be described or understood in the language of reason and sense experience. But it can be discussed and understood and related to. It is the realm about which all religions have spoken. Indeed, it is my suggestion that this is one of the primary functions of religion, to offer understanding of this reality which moves and acts in the heart of being, and that Christianity is no exception.

I am also convinced, from studying other religions and mythologies, that Christianity can do this with greater depth and realism than any other religion. We must remember that just as there are destructive spiritual realities, so there are destructive myths. It makes a real difference for one's life which mythology attracts his allegiance. When the Christian story is understood as revealing most fully the nature of spiritual reality, it offers just as much help to confused man as it ever has. But to do this Christianity needs its myths. Myth is not to be rejected, but understood. With the help of its myth, as a respectable way of dealing with reality, this religion of ours can come alive again with power.

It is no easy matter, however, to change one's view of the world. Even when people are seeking some new way to believe, they find it difficult to see themselves surrounded by spiritual reality, and to understand that myth speaks of their encounter with this reality. To make a bridgehead, let's first of all look at a part of history which is known to all of us and see how myth was at work in the deaths of Abraham Lincoln and John Kennedy. Then let's consider briefly the main threads of myth in relation to men's understanding of evil, and go on to relate the specific myths of the dying and rising god. Next we shall see how Christianity carries this essential myth into history. With this background we'll go more deeply into the meaning of myth and see how far this fits with our best and most developed thinking about man and his world. At this point we take a page out of science to correct our one-sided theology. Finally we shall consider practical suggestions for getting into the meaning of myth today, and for making the Christian myth a living, transforming, vitally renewing power in our lives in the modern world. Learning to think in the images of myths changes lives spiritually, mentally, and even physically.

II
Myth
in History

If myth is as much alive as we suggest, then we should be able to spot its effects in the pages of history without much trouble. To see if this is true, let us look at the assassinations of two American presidents and the effect these two events had on the American people. We find that, far from being an unreality or something untouchable, one of the oldest and best known myths of mankind is still being lived out in our midst.

In the deaths of Abraham Lincoln and John Fitzgerald Kennedy the myth of the dying god broke forth with striking power to play upon the lives of millions of Americans. In these two events, that original pattern, which was familiar in ancient times, suddenly reappeared in space and time and was recorded in the annals of United States history in ways that are still fearfully alive in the memories of many of us. The very depth of people was touched. We apparently even altered aspects of the lives of these men, reshaping them where they did not fit into the pattern. In fact, one book that deals with many of these facts was originally entitled "The Dying God." This is the fascinating *Myths after Lincoln* by Lloyd Lewis, which was written with the encouragement of Carl Sandburg. Let us outline the pattern of these events as they happened, and then look at each of these lives in more detail.

Both Lincoln and Kennedy were inaugurated in the sixty-first year of their centuries. Both were shot on a Friday by an unstable person caught up by the inner world. Each of the assassins was himself slain by someone who thought that he was doing God's will in this act of retribution. There was an immediate response on the part of nearly all Americans, and even those who had been violently hostile before were overcome by grief. There then followed two of the largest and most impressive funerals ever held in America, and as the reactions of millions poured out, unusual events began to be noted. Something deep and meaningful was touched in the American psyche. Deep called unto deep.

Thus briefly the myth stood out, first in death, and then in the emotions and the imagination of a whole people. By the time the tragedies had been absorbed and men were turning back to ordinary concerns, their lives had been changed and the course of history altered. The myth had been played out. We turn now to look at the pattern of mythological significance in the lives in which it had moved.

The Myth in Lincoln's Life

The inner realities which moved Lincoln's life were far from simple. Lincoln was a self-made man. He had never been close to his father, but he had been close first to his own mother who died, and then to his stepmother for whom he continued to have deep and real affection. Certainly Lincoln had a positive and creative relation to each of these women who was mother to him. He was a rare combination of the best and deepest feminine qualities along with real masculinity. If we can lay aside the current prejudice that a man's close relation to the mother always means subjection, and necessarily produces a negative complex, this becomes clear. Lincoln's greatest characteristics were probably his humility and charity, his genuine self-effacement, and also his real love and concern for ordinary people.

Lincoln was also a very intuitive person. He took his dreams very seriously, as the following material shows, and he was in contact with a deep level of reality within himself. He also believed that he had a destiny. The first of his dreams that I quote occurred only days before his assassination on Good Friday, April 14, 1865. The evening on which Lincoln told his dream to a few friends remained a vivid memory to his former partner who set down the President's own words:

> "It seems strange," he said slowly, as though feeling for the words, "how much there is in the Bible about dreams. There are, I think, some sixteen chapters in the Old Testament and four or five in the New in which dreams are mentioned; and there are many other passages scattered throughout the book which refer to visions. If we believe the Bible, we must accept the fact that, in the old days, God and his angels came to men in their sleep and made themselves known in dreams."

> Mr. Lincoln studied the suddenly solemn faces of his friends. He sat forward, elbows on knees, the veined hands describing small gestures.

> "Nowadays," he said apologetically, "dreams are regarded as very foolish, and are seldom told, except by old women and by young men and maidens in love."

> Mrs. Lincoln looked worried. "Why?" she said. "Do you believe in dreams?"

> "I can't say that I do," he said, hedging against the nightmares she had suffered for many years, "but I had one the other night which has haunted me ever

since. After it occurred, the first time I opened the Bible, strange as it may appear, it was at the twenty-eighth chapter of Genesis, which relates the wonderful dream Jacob had. I turned to other passages, and seemed to encounter a dream or a vision wherever I looked. I kept on turning the leaves of the old book, and everywhere my eyes fell upon passages recording matters strangely in keeping with my own thoughts— supernatural visitations, dreams, visions, and so forth."

Mrs. Lincoln clutched her bosom. "You frighten me," she breathed. "What is the matter?"

At once the President tried to dismiss it. "I am afraid," he said, "that I have done wrong to mention the subject at all. But somehow, the thing has gotten possession of me, and, like Banquo's ghost, it will not down...." [And as Mrs. Lincoln demanded to hear the dream, he went on.]

"About ten days ago, I retired very late. I had been waiting up for important dispatches. I could not have been long in bed when I fell into a slumber, for I was weary. I soon began to dream. There seemed to be a deathlike stillness about me. Then I heard subdued sobs, as if a number of people were weeping. I thought I left my bed and wandered downstairs.

"There the silence was broken by the same pitiful sobbing, but the mourners were invisible. I went from room to room. No living person was in sight, but the same mournful sounds of distress met me as I passed along. It was light in all the rooms; every object was familiar to me, but where were all the people who were grieving as if their hearts would break?

"I was puzzled and alarmed. What could be the meaning of all this? Determined to find the cause of a state of things so mysterious and so shocking, I kept on until I arrived in the East Room, which I entered.

There I met with a sickening surprise. Before me was
a catafalque, on which rested a corpse in funeral vestments. Around it were stationed soldiers who were
acting as guards; and there was a throng of people,
some gazing mournfully upon the corpse, whose face
was covered, others weeping pitifully.

" 'Who is dead in the White House?' I demanded
of one of the soldiers.

" 'The President,' was his answer. 'He was killed
by an assassin.'

"Then came a loud burst of grief from the crowd,
which awoke me from my dream. I slept no more that
night, and, although it was only a dream, I have been
strangely annoyed by it ever since."[1]

Ward Hill Lamon from whom this story comes was
not one of the biographers who tried to romanticize Lincoln. Indeed his biography was so down-to-earth and factual that it did not sell well, for the public wanted a more
perfect figure than this friend and bodyguard of Lincoln
described. The second volume of the work which he had
projected was never completed because the first had been
so poorly received. Even so, this is one of the best historical
sources we have for the life of Lincoln.

Lamon and others told of two other occasions on which
the President had particularly remarked on dream experiences. One was recalled by various cabinet members
who attended the last meeting of Lincoln's cabinet on
Good Friday, a few hours before his assassination. When
Grant, who was a guest at the meeting that afternoon,
"had worried about Sherman, down in North Carolina,
Lincoln had said that he felt everything would be all
right since he had had, last night, the dream which always
came to him before important events in the war—the
dream in which he was in a mysterious vessel 'sailing
toward a dark and indefinite shore.' "[2] Apparently he

spoke of this twice during the meeting.

The other experience, which may have been a vision or a dream, occurred just after Lincoln's first election in 1860. John Hay, who was later ambassador to Great Britain, was one of the principal sources for the account of this dream experience. Lincoln had been receiving the news and the acclaim of well-wishers in Springfield when, as he told,

"... I was well tired out and went home to rest, throwing myself on a lounge in my chamber. Opposite to where I lay there was a bureau with a swinging glass in it, and looking in that glass I saw myself reflected at nearly full length; but my face, I noticed, had two separate and distinct images, the tip of the nose of one being about three inches from the tip of the other. I was a little bothered, perhaps startled, and got up and looked in the glass, but the illusion vanished. On lying down again, I saw it a second time, plainer if possible, than before; and then I noticed that one of the faces was a little paler—say, five shades —than the other.

"I got up and the thing melted away, and I went off, and in the excitement of the hour forgot all about it—nearly, but not quite, for the thing would come up once in a while and give me a little pang as though something disagreeable had happened. . . . A few days after I tried the experiment again, when, sure enough, the thing came back again; but I never succeeded in bringing the ghost back after that, though once I tried very industriously to show it to my wife, who was worried about it somewhat. She thought it a sign that I was to be elected to a second term of office and that the paleness of one of the faces was an omen that I should not see life throughout the last term."[3]

Whatever our particular insight into these events from

out of the unconscious, they cannot be termed mere chance productions. Dreams and visions do appear from time to time which have just this startling relationship to actual future happenings that are only beginning to take shape as possibilities. These psychic events which foreshadow the future spring from that unexplained reality found in the depth of man.

Just before Lincoln was elected there was another dreamer who had foreseen the whole tragedy of civil war and had done the only thing he knew to forestall it. This was John Brown, who had a prophetic vision of blood rising in gulfs to drown his country. Those who have read Jung's profound and fascinating autobiography, *Memories, Dreams, Reflections,* are undoubtedly reminded of the similar dream which came to Jung just before World War I. But in John Brown's fanatic consciousness there had also risen a dream of keeping the sea from overflowing the land by dipping out a handful of this red water.

If Lincoln had not undertaken the heroic task of keeping his country together, we can hardly imagine what the course of modern history might have been; yet he did succeed. Through his quiet and seemingly bungling way he had accomplished his task. During the week before his assassination Lee had surrendered. This was Lincoln's hour of victory. Grant had come to Washington to celebrate with him the approaching end of the war. And then, in the moment for rejoicing, almost as if the gods were allowing the beloved to be struck down as in the myth of the dying god, Lincoln was slain. It had also been more than a moment for rejoicing. Lincoln had been planning the way to bring the Southern states back into the Union without humiliation. In the moment of preparing for a work of great charity, he was assassinated.

On the day of his death the Washington *Evening Star* was adding to the festive spirit by talking about Lincoln's intended visit to Ford's Theatre. Strangely, at almost the

same hour of that afternoon the *Whig Press* of Middle-
town, New York, was publishing the news that the
President had been shot. As Jim Bishop has pointed out
in his factual account, *The Day Lincoln Was Shot,* the
sources of this "news" were never discovered, nor was it
found out why the editors published the story without
first checking with Washington. That same afternoon the
people of Manchester, New Hampshire, were buzzing with
rumors about an attempt on President Lincoln's life, and
in what was then the remote town of St. Joseph, Minnesota, forty miles from the nearest telegraph office, people gathered on the street before dark to talk about the
"news" that the President had been slain. The event was
in the air even before it occurred. The myth was alive.

Lincoln himself was more than a little naive about his
own protection. Like many men with a positive mother
complex, he accepted his fate and did not try to determine
it. At the theatre that night he apparently took no notice
of the fact that his bodyguard had become bored by listening at the door and had gone out for a drink. Yet
John Parker was not there to keep the assassin out. Even
though the secret service had been informed of a plot to
kidnap the President—a plot which John Wilkes Booth
had actually considered—they had not taken it seriously.
The door was simply left open for tragedy.

In Booth we find another life almost as complicated
and tragic as that of John Kennedy's assassin. He too had
a mother complex, but unlike Lincoln's relation to the
mother, this was a negative, a destructive one. Booth had
been so pampered by his mother and the other women of
the family that he had never learned to work. His acting
was successful only because he had an appeal for the less
discerning people of fashion, most of them women with
romantic ideas. It seems probable that he planned and
executed the act of murder because he wanted to be as-
sured of a place in history. While history has narrowly

missed judging this man insane, he was most likely what we would call a borderline psychopath.

Booth's own death came at the hands of a man who had been given explicit orders not to kill him. Washington had the idea that Booth was only the front for a large-scale Confederate plot, and the government wanted him kept alive at all costs. When a detachment of soldiers finally cornered him, there was only one shot. A religious fanatic, Sergeant Boston Corbett, suddenly found that he was ordained of God to avenge the murder of the President. He took uncanny aim through a crack in the wall, killing Booth with one bullet in the back of the head in almost the same spot in which Lincoln had been struck. "God Almighty directed me," was Corbett's ready answer when he was questioned, and no action was taken for his disobedience of orders.

Lincoln's funeral procession was one of the greatest spectacles America had ever seen. Behind the engine which had first brought the newly elected President to Washington, the funeral train took the body north as far as Albany, and then from town to town across the country to Chicago, and supposedly its last resting place in Springfield. All along the route crowds lined the tracks. From Baltimore on, city after city was hung with black crepe and wreaths, vying for the most elaborate expression of grief.

New York was only one of the cities that held a parade complete with floats and floral monuments and inscribed banners overhead. In the Indianapolis State House, in a huge, dark room pillared with portraits of the country's great men, the casket was viewed under a black velvet canopy sprinkled with gold stars. Chicago was draped in black, from the statues to the gloves of policemen and children. Through city after city the body moved under arches of flowers and transplanted trees.

Spring had come early that year, and with the countryside in bloom as rarely happened, the train itself became a floral tribute; the moment a bloom wilted there were ten more to take its place. And the crowds increased at the same rate as people moved on ahead of the train hoping to catch another glimpse of the body in the next city. Thousands, often hundreds of thousands, thronged past the casket at every stop. Everywhere groups of women costumed in symbolic black and white met the train, choirs poured out hymns, tears were shed, and dreams intended and unintended were enacted. From pulpits all up and down the country Lincoln was compared to the Christ, and the flood of eulogies was met with an almost incredible release of emotion. Tragically, however, the people were moved towards vengeance rather than to the spirit of their avowed hero.

If the weeping and wailing across the nation are hard to believe, there is an even stranger story in the movements of Lincoln's body after it came to Springfield. From the receiving vault in which it was first placed, the body was moved eleven times before it finally rested ten feet underground in a steel and concrete cage in Oak Ridge Cemetery outside Springfield. Seven times the lead casket had to be cut open; seven times it was officially verified that Lincoln's body was there, and the plumber's assistant, Leon P. Hopkins, dutifully sealed it up again. Whether there was a secret hope that here would be another empty tomb, or whether it was fear that the body had really been stolen, is hard to decide. Perhaps both reasons played a part.

There was a plot to steal Lincoln's body and ransom it back to the government, which was discovered by detectives and stopped as the casket was being removed from its crypt. In the end, a group of self-appointed custodians, who called themselves the "Guard of Honor," actually did remove the body in secret. One of their members was the official custodian of the memorial hall which had been built to house it. For many years people who came to visit it paid their respects to an empty tomb, while this group moved the body from place to place in the connecting catacombs. Finally in 1901 the casket was opened a last time before being sealed irrevocably in tons of reinforced concrete deep underneath the huge marble monument.

The Myth Embroidered

Long before this the myth had begun to envelop Lincoln himself. Tales began to grow up around him almost immediately after his death. The only books about him which were not a success were those that told the truth as best it could be ascertained. Lamon's book, as we have mentioned, did not sell apparently because it pictured a man with faults and real heroism, rather than a demigod. Herndon, Lincoln's former partner, also produced a failure by writing what he knew of Lincoln and showing the elaborations for what they were.

There was story enough without elaboration. But what the people wanted was a myth complete, and there were other writers ready with all the trappings, whether they could be made to fit the reality or not. Stories circulated about the illegitimacy of Lincoln, and also of his mother's birth out of wedlock. Others told of the dignitary who had been his real father. His origins must have been either more humble or less humble than they really were. As the cabin in which he was born became poorer and smaller than it was, his birth became extraordinary. He was alive only because of the unaccountable visit of a neighbor who found the mother giving birth alone during a blizzard, although actually she had been well attended and the weather quiet. Nancy Lincoln's very pregnancy became a myth, with the picture of one long mystical experience which accounted for the bond between mother and son. Even Lincoln's own traits, his melancholy and his human sympathy, were often laid solely to his dreams, without any regard for the facts of the time or the possible effect of his being married to an excitable wife.

It was not long before tales began to circulate around Booth as well. Because of the way in which the government quickly secreted his body and buried it away, rumors soon rose that Booth had never been captured but was still at large, and over the years there were various persons who claimed to be the missing assassin. Around him the story arose that, like Cain and Judas, John Wilkes Booth was condemned to live on and wander, being unable to die.

Meanwhile neither the churches nor the opponents of religion were backward about demonstrating the religious quality of this search for the myth in Lincoln's life. He was described as a very religious man, and he was depicted as an atheist. He was claimed by sect after sect with stories to support a secret allegiance to some article of faith, and details of a later conversion to an orthodox Christianity were repeated in numerous versions. On the other side men like Robert Ingersoll were equally positive about Lincoln's stand against religion. The people were fast trying to lose the man in the myth which his life represented for them. And one more tale was told from time to time; his body had petrified or turned to stone. . . .

The truth of the matter is that Lincoln was a religious man, but not because of his contact with the churches of the time. For the most part they were rigid institutions, doctrinally correct, but with little life or compassion, mainly interested in keeping their people out of the human depths. In fact, the major denominations even found it possible to avoid the issue of slavery almost entirely until it had been settled by the nation.

While there were probably more reasons than one why Lincoln never joined any church, and even avoided them in his earlier years, his religious devotion was genuine. He had a detailed knowledge of the Bible, and apparently read it daily. He was also a man of prayer, one who knew the deep inner reaches of the soul and communed with the power which one finds when he turns inward. In the end, the attempt to make him into an orthodox Christian, in the mold of the time, was no more successful than any of the other attempts to nourish the myth with untruths. It represented, not the real Lincoln, but rather a failure on the part of the church. The real myth lay in the life of the real Lincoln.

Whatever else one may find in these various facets of the Lincoln story, it is quite clear that something of greater than ordinary power broke through into history in his life. A mythological pattern which men had dreamed of since the dawn of time was reenacted. And for the most part it took place on the American political scene, in full view of the whole people, barely a hundred years ago. As the myth of the dying god broke forth in these events, it struck at the deepest religious level of the people and aroused in them religious feelings of which they had been unaware, religious feelings which their formal religion had left untouched.

The Myth in Our Time

We are still so close to the Kennedy assassination, and its echo in the killing of Robert Kennedy, that it is more difficult to consider objectively. For my own part, I had not been a Kennedy supporter. I had felt that he was identifying too much with the role that had come to him. And yet, like a great many others, I was as moved through those sad days as his most ardent followers. In John Kennedy's death and the experiences that surrounded it, something mythological broke through, something which was felt by the whole people, reaching to the very roots of their being.

Many of the same motifs or patterns were present in

this situation that had appeared in the history of Lincoln. Kennedy was closer to his mother than to his father, and she is clearly a woman of tremendous strength.[4] Here again we find a son who had the power and compassion that so often result from a positive mother complex, and besides this both parents had great ambitions for their children. His older brother, who was killed in the war, had first been destined in their minds to become president. John Kennedy then became a war hero himself and also a teller of tales of heroism. He was already capturing the popular imagination with his *Profiles in Courage,* and by his marriage shortly after entering the Senate. In the presidential campaign he showed as brilliant a mind as Lincoln's, and as readily touched with humor. He too captained the ship of state through deeply troubled times, with one crisis after another from Berlin to Cuba.

I remember well the remark of a very intuitive friend of mine, who said early that he doubted if Kennedy would finish out his term. He pointed up the fact of his brother's death, his narrow achieving of the nomination, his apparent feeling of having been destined to be president, and then the very small margin by which he was finally elected. Like most men with a mother complex (and realize that this is not condemnatory), he was contemptuous of his own safety, feeling almost as if powers greater than he would be caring for him. Much the same attitude also seemed to guide many of the actions of Robert Kennedy during his tragic campaign for the presidency a few years later. There is real danger in this reliance on the "mother."

John Kennedy often slipped away from the secret service men just as Lincoln had done, making very nearly a game of it. Had he used the plastic bubble on his car that day, he might still be alive. He too was killed on a Friday. As he slumped in Jackie Kennedy's arms, the picture left almost an imprint of Michelangelo's "Pietà," the unfor-

gettable image of the crucified Son in Mary's arms.
Through television his funeral was witnessed by more
people than any other funeral in all history. People sat
glued to their TV sets, held there by a power they could
scarcely understand. The myth was alive; it grasped them
at the heart and would not let them go.

An amazing web of coincidence began to appear to
connect Kennedy with Lincoln, beginning with the general concern of both men with the civil rights issue. It is
pointed out that both men were succeeded by vice-presi-
dents named Johnson, who were Southern Democrats,
both former members of the Senate, and both born in the
same year of their centuries, 1808 and 1908. The assassins
in each case, both of whom were shot and died instantly
before they could be tried, were also Southerners born in
the same year of their centuries, Booth in 1839 and Oswald in 1939. During their term of office each of these
two presidents had lost a son by death. And each had gone
against the advice of his personal secretary in going to the
place where he was assassinated; in Lincoln's case it was
a Mr. Kennedy who tried to persuade him not to go to the
theatre that evening, while John Kennedy's secretary,
who felt he should not be in Dallas on that Friday a hundred years later, was Mrs. Lincoln.

Two other coincidences occurred around the death of
Kennedy which may have mythological significance. The
first of these was recorded by John Ciardi in the *Saturday
Review*. He was describing the events of his own day on a
Friday in 1963, the day on which Kennedy was to die.

As I walked through the office to my cubbyhole,
[he wrote] Mary Harvey handed me a copy of the December *Redbook,* opened to an article she had been
reading. "Look at this," she said. The article by Jhan
Robbins was a compilation of answers given by European children to a series of questions about American
life. The first question was also the title of the article:

"What are Americans like?" The first four sentences
of the first answer to that question read:
"The average American is, of course, a Texan. He
eats lots of breakfast and gets fat so he has to go on a
diet because he likes to look skinny. He calls everyone
'sweetheart' and is bad to colored people. If he doesn't
like who is his President, he usually shoots him."[5]

Perhaps this was only a bit of coincidence. Or perhaps
there was an unconscious connection of some kind. Call it
happenstance or meaningful coincidence—synchronicity,
as Jung has termed it—such a meaningful connection was
made in the minds of many people. Several persons called
my attention to the timing of the article and the fact that
such a well-known critic had commented on it.

The other account appeared in Paul Coate's column in
The Los Angeles Times for February 28, 1964, three
months after the assassin, Lee Harvey Oswald, had been
caught with the rifle that fired the shots. This story read:

A note in the mail from Mrs. Clifton Fadiman.
She writes that their ten year old, Anne, is a student
at Westlake School.

Her sixth grade class is working with a grammar
textbook titled: "Easy English Exercises," new edi-
tion. Publishers—Harcourt, Brace and World, Inc.,
New York, Atlanta, Chicago, Burlingame and Dallas.

It was that mention of Dallas that took on a special, eerie quality for the Fadimans' youngster when,
the other day, she turned to an exercise question on
page 81, sentence 19.

It read: "The clear proof of Oswald's guilt now
lay before us."

Copyright date of "Easy English Exercises"? All
right, I'll tell you. First copyright, 1935. Second, 1956.

It's a good thing that our little group around here

doesn't go in for any of that metaphysical jazz. Could really unnerve you.

As Mrs. Fadiman, a very charming, calm, competent journalist in her own right, wrote me, "It is nothing more than a chilling coincidence."

But, chilling it is!

Kennedy's assassin was actually similar in many ways to Booth, but without even Booth's success in a career. Here was a man whose relation to the mother was completely negative. Oswald was deeply in touch with the inner world and with a destructive mother complex that colored everything in it. He lived out the destructive phantasies of that world, the evil in it. As in one ancient story of the dying god, he acted out the role of the destroyer—the wild boar that gores Adonis, striking without even knowing why. We shall never know all of Oswald's outer motives, for his was a lonely plot, and he had said little about it. But evidently he had felt that it was his destiny to slay the president. He was known to be a president hater and the secret service had not acted to forestall him.

Lincoln's murder had been followed by an attempt to kill Seward, the Secretary of State, who narrowly missed losing his life, and only the cringing fear of a third amateur accomplice had saved Andrew Johnson from a similar attack. Oswald also killed and killed again; the governor of Texas narrowly missed being his second victim, and in attempting to escape he shot and killed another innocent bystander, a citizen by the name of Tibbits. Like Booth, Oswald too was slain by a man who felt himself appointed by God to avenge the President's murder; Jack Ruby, who shot Oswald in full view of the television audience, was himself moved by a deep level of the collective unconscious, the inner primal world.

Here, in each of these men forces are seen at work which do not belong just to the known human world of emotions and desires and humanly willed actions working together with consciousness. There were deep primal patterns at work which usually lie at rest within the polite forms of a culture. Here we have seen them break forth in complex ways; even the adulation which Kennedy has received since his death speaks of forces beyond the ordinary. What other man's death has been so quickly and thoroughly capitalized on, with images of all kinds? Within two months anyone with $5.88 to spare could own a memorial bust of John Kennedy, or for the going rate a coin with his bas-relief.[6]

Kennedy's dreams are not known to us, nor do we know of any premonitions that may have come to him. I do know, however, of the dreams of two friends which were unusual to them and seemed related to the event in Dallas. One was the dream of a young man who was counseling with me, which occurred on Thursday night before the assassination. In it he saw the Capitol in Washington shaken by a mighty earthquake and watched it fall in rubble to the ground. Another friend, a mature man who lives across the country, wrote to me of his dreaming on that same night about a candle which was being broken and torn apart. He awoke from the dream in a state of tension which frightened him, since it persisted through the morning. When he heard that the President had been shot, the tension was suddenly resolved and he knew the meaning of the dream.

These "vibrations of John F. Kennedy's approaching assassination appeared to hang electrically in the air," as Jess Stearn, one of the leading writers on psychic experiences today, has noted. He describes the foreboding that greeted the President's decision to go to Dallas. One well-known psychic medium, the late Florence Sternfels who lived in Edgewater, New Jersey, begged everyone who called her to get in touch with the FBI and ask them not to let him go to Texas. Helen Stalls in New York is another widely known psychic adviser who spoke out that the President was about to be shot, and later predicted Robert Kennedy's death in the same way. "There are times," the author suggests, "when an event is so surely destined that the vibration of that event almost overwhelms the psychic with its intensity."[7]

On the day of Kennedy's death, it was also reported in the television newscasts that a woman in Los Angeles had contacted Washington that morning, trying to get someone to listen to a dream she had just had. She had been awakened by a sequence of images in which she saw the President slain, and was trying to give a warning. But she had not found anyone willing to listen to what was apparently just the story of another crackpot.

Here again, in the death of this president and in the events of the week that followed, is the ancient story, the myth of the dying and rising god. Can anyone who actually lived through these events question the power of this myth in our lives? We have only to remember the almost ghostly participation through television, the partaking by a whole nation in one long ritual of grief, which helped each of us to face and even to act upon our own fears and hopes. Primitive cultures once practiced the ritual murder of their kings, and even included human sacrifice as a part of the rite. These rituals made the myth of the dying and rising god live and somehow renewed the people and gave them new life. In the tragedy of John Kennedy the American people experienced something very similar.

Five years later the sequence was enacted once more, in images that came first into an unbalanced mind, and then onto the television screen, and millions of us watched in horror as Robert Kennedy lay dying on the floor of a Los Angeles hotel. Once again the patterns were the same. In this younger Kennedy there was the same closeness to the mother, with a warmth and concern for human problems, the same disregard for personal safety. Again there was the acclaim of victory—the victory that could well have meant nomination for the presidency—and within moments he had been shot and five others wounded. His assassin, Sirhan, was a man completely dominated by his own phantasies, at home only in an inner world, a world of mirror images. As one friend remarked, the elements were all reflected; the shooting even took place in an area called the "Mirror Room." Yet this time the tragedy seemed to be more a personal one, and probably fewer people felt touched by the forces that had broken through again into present-day lives.

We have seen in these particular moments of history—as in hundreds of others that could be described—how the powers of death and destruction can break through the mind of an unbalanced man in mythological patterns. Something beyond these men uses them as a tool, thus emerging to leave an imprint on the history of a whole people. In these particular stories it is easy to see how the course of our own history has been changed. Later we shall consider how the same kind of power erupted in Nazi Germany.

As I have watched these things happening in our time, and felt my own reactions and the reactions of those around me, realizing that we are seeing age-old myths unfold before our eyes, I have wondered what hope there is for man to deal with powers like these. I have realized that this is a matter of salvation, and that salvation is one thing about which our religion has quite a bit to say.

The basic idea of Christianity is that Christians are given a way to deal with these destructive powers. In a very real way the same powers, the very ones that destroyed Lincoln and both John and Robert Kennedy, converged on Christ and tried to destroy him. But he conquered them and gave to his followers a way to deal with them. If these primal spiritual forces—these archetypal powers both good and evil—can work through the collective unconscious of man to influence history, and if we have the ability to touch and influence them through our myth and ritual and imagination, including imaginative prayer, then we can in actual fact alter the course of history. The myth that men really believe in allows them to approach these powers. And the Christian story shows us how we can touch them, both in ourselves and in other men. It suggests very clearly how we can become aware of these forces and sort them out, and how we can confront the destructive ones so as not to be swamped by them. This is the message we shall be considering.

In order to see the importance of our own Christian understanding, let us first see what other religious approaches there are to this problem which affects all men whether they know it or not.

III

Myth and the
Problem of Evil

Modern man is probably more aware of the evil going on in the world than ever before in history. Mass media make it possible for the day's news to flow right through his living room, and destructiveness and tragedy have news value. Kidnappings, mass murders, political assassinations, and skyjackings are fascinating. The average citizen of the twentieth century may spend his hard-earned cash to inspect the blood-spattered Ford in which Bonnie and Clyde died. But he still doesn't want to look directly at the possibility that these evils spring from a principle, a center or source of evil that might touch any one of us. There is real resistance even to looking at the question, let alone seriously considering it.

There are a number of reasons for this reticence, but we do not have to look far to find two of the most important ones. First of all, secular man in this century has been brainwashed by materialistic thought. In a rational and materialistic world there is no place for such a principle of destructiveness. It is neither rational nor material, and so it cannot exist. If one is to consider the possibility that evil is something more substantial than just the absence of good, then he has to overhaul his whole world view, and this is a very painful and difficult task. It is better simply to deny the reality of any such principle out of hand.

The second reason is a little more complex. Man feels he has a right to enjoy what is good in the world. If evil actually exists as something more than chance, more than an accidental, temporary failure in the continually evolving perfection of the world, then one has something rather fearful to deal with. If man should discover a demonic, destructive reality at work in the world, then he has reason to fear, and he needs to find some way of dealing with it. And this involves religion and responsibility. If such a reality exists and there is a way of dealing with it, then man has a moral responsibility, and this interferes with his right of full enjoyment. Men of all ages shirk this whenever they can. It is easier and nicer just to think that there is nothing there. Then we don't have to look and get involved in a moral obligation.

The New Testament and the Christianity which emerges from its pages offer a completely different idea about the nature of evil. From start to finish the Christian message is concerned with elements of evil in the basic structure of man's world, and it presents a very specific picture of the problem. Evil is *not* seen as something that happens simply in the outer world, which men can only deal with piecemeal. It is *not* considered something that occurs merely by chance, or just because the physical world is made that way. Instead, evil is considered to be a force standing in opposition to God. It is essentially a pattern of reality emanating from the spiritual world which infects men and influences them, detouring them from God and tearing them down morally, mentally and physically. It also inflicts various kinds of damage on the physical world. Evil then is seen as a reality, subsisting apart from the world, but entering into it and working through men and their ordinary day-to-day world.

It is seen, however, as a reality which can be overcome by men when they turn to God for help. This view contrasts sharply with the Hebrew tradition which regarded evil elements as scapegoats, to be driven out of man's life and then ignored as best he could.[1] In this light the focus of the New Testament becomes very clear. It is concentrated on helping men recognize and deal with these patterns of reality, these spiritual forces of evil which were called demons, Satan, and by several other names. The Christian view assumes that man will have sense enough to make the effort and keep an alert eye on them. Then he can expect some help beyond just his own moral ability to resist them.

Although this mythological understanding of evil is not regarded very favorably by sophisticated people today, it is often expressed, at least in part, in popular ways. Evil is taken quite seriously in the movies and on the television screen, and men like Rollo May who are investigating violence in our society seem to recognize that there is some kind of reality in images of evil. Literature of all kinds, from Goethe's *Faust* to *Frankenstein* and *Dracula,* speaks of confronting and defeating evil. This was Shakespeare's theme in *Hamlet, Macbeth, King Lear,* and very likely his early work *Venus and Adonis* expressed the elements of his own personal struggle with evil. *Venus and Adonis* deals with one of the myths of the dying and rising god which we shall discuss in the next chapter.

In recent years there have been increasing evidences of the reality of evil. The best-seller novel *The Exorcist,* for instance, was based on a real case of possession, and there was nothing fictional at all about the satanic impulses of the Manson "family," or about the facts recorded in Truman Capote's book *In Cold Blood*—or, for that matter, about Dachau and Buchenwald. The only thing unreal about the smell of burning flesh coming from the crematoriums in 1940* was the fact that such things could happen among the decent, hard-working, moral citizens of Germany.

---

*Fifteen concentration camps were operating in Germany by 1942.

Yet we Westerners do not seem to have grown much wiser after two world wars and a dozen minor ones, in which there were events almost too terrible to describe. We have not really learned that we all become instruments of evil when wrongs like these are perpetrated. Instead, we seem to feel that there is an immunity in innocence from evil. It need not work in us if we simply believe that it has no reality—at least none which man could not control perfectly well if he would just make up his mind to do so and would use his best scientific techniques. For peoples who profess to hold such a belief, we have taken quite an interest in ways of inflicting evil on others.

Other Myths of Evil

Obviously the Christian myth is not the only one at work in our world today. If we are to have some idea of what choice is offered, we need to look at other approaches which have been developed from man's myths and see the ways they offer understanding of the world around us. In this way one may be able to draw some conclusions of his own about these various points of view. Besides the Christian approach, there are six of these basic mythological views which we shall consider. Later we shall ask which of them comes closest to expressing the actual nature of the world, both physical and spiritual, in which we live.

Perhaps it seems strange to distinguish between these points of view principally on the basis of how they approach evil. Why not ask first of all how they differ about God? The real reason is that only the most primitive religions try to describe God specifically. We can speak of the nature of God only as we see him in relationship to the rest of the universe. The problem of evil is for man a very important part of that universe. If we are to learn how to find and know God in this world, then we must be willing to become conscious enough to face the activity of evil in it, the disruptions and destructiveness which make the form of God show up with some clarity. And it is on the very subject of evil that some of the greatest differences exist between various religious points of view.

Besides this, each of these religious approaches has a real contribution to make to religious practice and understanding, Christian and otherwise. I am not trying to show that Christianity should exclude all other points of view and prove them to be without merit. As John S. Dunne has made so clear in *The Way of All the Earth,*[2] the fact is that we Christians can learn a great deal from other religions. On the other hand, our interest here is to distinguish the unique values in Christianity, and there *are* differences, many of them relating to the problem of evil. Briefly, then—although any one of these myths could well fill a book or two—let us start with what is unquestionably the predominant view of our time, the view which must be termed the "myth of materialism."

Materialism and Evil

The idea of materialism as a religious point of view may surprise some people, and it may shock others even more to speak of materialism as a myth. Yet this understanding—the idea that matter and the energy that pervades it are the only realities in the universe—is as much a matter of faith as any kind of belief in God,[3] and this idea has provided a great many modern men with their central reason for being and acting. For instance, in Russia this belief provides the central motivation, apparently individual as well as social and political, for a rather large-scale operation which has made efforts to erase all other beliefs from men's minds.

Since the belief in materialism seems to have far-reaching effects beyond the good things that have resulted, it is fortunate that the implications of this point of view have been drawn out point by point by one of its leading spokesmen. B. F. Skinner believes that, in the last analysis, there is only matter to deal with, and that man is just an extended complexity of matter, another material thing. Man's ultimate concern must be to build a utopia of material things with himself as the center of it. All of Skinner's works have pointed towards the practical means of achieving this goal. He considers that the prime need is to bring man's behavior, and thus his whole outlook, into line, and that this can be achieved through "operant conditioning" by rewarding "good" behavior, very much like training the reflexes of some animal in a circus show.

In his last work, *Beyond Freedom and Dignity,* Skinner leaves no doubt about the results of this system for human life. There is certainly no place in it for radical evil, or for any other spiritual realities, which might awaken men to ask questions. If they believed in a spiritual realm, they might even consider themselves important, as channels of communication from that realm. But according to this point of view, the worst thing that men can do is to think that they have this kind of value and meaning. They then become vain and resist submitting to the necessary conditioning. The need is for docile subjects who will cooperate in this process so as to produce a happy life for the whole group. Konrad Lorenz comes to essentially the same conclusion in his naturalistic study *On Aggression.*

In fact, this is about as close as the materialist comes to thinking about evil. Evil, the materialist believes, is anything that stands in the way of man's efforts to achieve a materialistic utopia. According to this point of view his ideas about spiritual reality are simply illusions, but when they get in man's way and make him resist what is good for him, these ideas actually become evil in themselves. This is far from the original Christian understanding of a force or pattern of evil independent of man and the material world, putting its imprint on them. For the materialist, evil results from an accidental lack of perfection in the immediate state of affairs. Yet who has imagination enough to consider the German concentration camp as only an accidental lack of perfection in an otherwise perfectible universe? And where the only reality is inert matter, there is real difficulty in confronting the problem of evil. One thinks he has hold of the problem, only to find it dissolving into a mist of conflicting forces.*

While this point of view appeals to many practical people, particularly practical scientists, it does not take in all the facts. If evil is only a thing of the moment, a practical impediment, man is left holding the bag with no free hand to deal with it. Of course, there is still another problem with this point of view: Who is to be trusted to determine what is to shape the utopian world?

The Point of View of the East

Half-way around the world, culturally as well as geographically, we find almost the opposite approach to man's religious problems. India is certainly one of the most fascinating and ancient of the world's melting pots. And the religious traditions of this land are also old and complex. Hinduism was already centuries old—a combination of local cults with the sacrificial religion of Aryan invaders—when the reformation by Gautama Buddha and his followers began about six hundred years before Christ. In almost every way the myths of these two religions contrast with materialism.

---

*The ancient Greek myth of Proteus, who came up from the sea and could only be captured by a ruse because he changed from one shape to another at will, spoke precisely to this difficulty, which the rational Greeks comprehended very well.

To both Hindu and Buddhist the physical world is illusion; the spiritual powers which surround man are the reality of the universe. But even these are only passing configurations, like the shifting patterns in a child's kaleidoscope. In Buddhism the image is one of contemplation. But in Hinduism the gods appear in a succession of incarnations; in the ascetic tradition the phallic symbol may be dominant, or in a modern Hindu temple the walls depict countless images of gods in motion. Everything is in flux. But this—and even the seeming polytheism—is only apparent.

This religious tradition states that at the heart of the universe is the God, to whom all the images belong, who joins good and evil. Yet one is not put ahead of the other. Good and evil are both necessary. They are the poles of reality, which balance one another, both of them aspects of the ultimate. Man finds his salvation through beholding the image of this truth within himself, and by then giving up his will. Since every part of the whole is necessarily working towards the resolution of perfect balance, the individual's task is to submit to this process and accept his place in it with perfect harmony. Evil is not to be fought against; it is to be accepted as a necessary part of things.

Each man must work through his karma—the just deserts of his actions in this life—in order to come at length to the bliss of Nirvana. But what is involved is not so much personal merit, or the lack of it, as simply overcoming the fact that one is human and has emotions. If one does good, or if he does evil, it is not because of his will or determination, but because good or evil has been ordained. Thus to come to the final, exalted state of Nirvana, the only way is for all passion and emotion, all illusion to die. One must give up even his individuality and merge into the harmony of perfect process. This is the goal. Alan Watts, who is a leading interpreter of this point of view, expresses it well in his book *The Two Hands of God*. Or one can stop and talk to the saffron-robed Hari Krishna people on the corner of any big city and hear the same ideas from converts from Iowa.

In countries where these myths of evil are believed it is not hard to spot their practical effects. The idea of helping those in need, or of having a program of social welfare or free hospitals, has never come from this point of view. It is common in the cities of India to see homeless sick people lying in the street, or to watch a body being hauled away to be burned. The sick, the poverty-stricken are considered to be living out the karma of a previous existence, and men should not interfere. Man's task is only to know and accept reality as it is, and to give up any resistance to it.

Of course it is important to perceive the realities and truths which this point of view opens up. Doing this provides insights and meaning which are valuable. But this is only part of the story. What is really important is to see that Christianity goes on to provide a way of dealing with these realities, of conquering evil through love and sacrificial action. The myths of ancient India give a very different point of view from the traditional Christian understanding. When these Eastern ideas are accepted without reflection, and grafted onto our Western traditions, it produces strange, exotic fruits indeed, which may even be poisonous.

The Great Mother Goddesses

The early mythology of most peoples in the warm climates of the world reminds us that nature, if it is looked at honestly, reveals something besides simply beauty and harmony. The idea that nature is all good is a projection of romanticism and hardly in keeping with reality. Rousseau's vision of the noble savage was a beautiful dream,

but it has little to do with the facts that anthropologists
find. The balance of either the forest or the sea depends
on death and on the strong feeding on the weak. Terror
and destruction, ugliness and relentless annihilation exist
in nature side by side with beauty and peace. Nature is
amoral, and the myths of the great nature goddesses or
the mother goddesses portray this view of evil.

Beginning with the most ancient images that were
formed with great breasts and a heavy belly, these symbols
and stories developed among most primitive peoples from
the south Pacific to the Near East and back. One of the
Aztec figures in the museum in Mexico City is a gigantic
image of the earth goddess, wearing a crown of skulls,
with the heavy figure of the mother who sustains and
nourishes and a mouth that devours. Other examples are
the goddess in Crete with a snake coiled in her lap, Isis
in Egypt with repellent animal breasts, stroking her child
with one hand and a cobra with the other, the frightful
Ti-âmat in Babylonia, trying to swallow the great god,
and in Greece the siren Circe surrounded by fanged animals. All of these speak of this aspect of life.

There are innumerable myths of these goddesses who
attract and destroy, who nourish and devour. As Marie-
Louise von Franz has shown, the same theme was developed in the fairy-tales of peoples all around the world.[4]
Very often the stories tell of a creature who must be killed
or destroyed or driven away. But at the same time, particularly among the Semitic peoples, and in Egypt and Greece,
the stories were told of how the goddess was propitiated
or satisfied and men could go on with their lives. In all of
them the evil is simply there, without a solution for it.
It exists in flesh and spirit, represented by a figure that
attracts and horrifies.

The extent of these stories among primitive peoples
makes me wonder if man's earliest religion was not an attempt to deal somehow with evil. This two-handedness of

nature seems to appear as a part of all reality, both physical and spiritual. For instance the earliest flood story, from the peoples next door to the Hebrews, tells of that obviously actual event being decided on by a council of the gods. As soon as the waters receded, the Babylonian Noah gathered wood and poured a sweet libation into kettles. And "the gods smelled the sweet savor . . . (and) gathered like flies over the sacrificer."[5] Then the great goodess Ishtar regretted what she had allowed to happen to her people, and the gods took their "Noah" by the hand and touched him and made him like a god.

This important little story, coming from before the dawn of men's written records, suggests that a new vision was being prepared out of the myths and images of the great mother goddess. When evil had been plumbed, and men had felt the depth of suffering, even the gods might be touched by sacrifice and feel for men's need. And from another direction the experiences of shamanism, found all over the world, pointed to the same thing. As the shamans confronted the destructive side of spiritual reality and experienced its pain and dismemberment, and yet survived, they were then able to return as "wounded healers" and help men with the evil side of nature. This is the reality described in many modern sources, including Mircea Eliade's *Shamanism,* the books of Carlos Castaneda, John Neihardt's *Black Elk Speaks,* and Laurens van der Post's *A Story Like the Wind.* How these books have captured the imagination of today's college students, disenchanted as they are with modern society's superficial attitude towards spirit and evil.

In both of these ways, through the mother goddesses and through shamanism, we see the beginnings of the myth of the dying and rising god, as men faced intolerable evil and sought ways of dealing with it. Strangely, the two experiences came from poles apart; from the mother goddesses came the idea of outer sacrifice, while the

shamanistic vision and practice usually arose spontaneously as men began to deal with their inner darkness as
well as its outer counterparts.

The Myth of Power

In the myth of Wotan, which people thought was dead,
we find the strong god of the forest who would have his
way no matter what. He rode the winds followed by the
Valkyries, and wove spells over men, enrapturing them,
or driving them to frenzy in battle. What he willed was
right because he was power, ultimate power which has no
interest in justice. To identify with Wotan, to believe in
a universe governed by such a god, means believing that
might makes right, and that the will of the strong must
dominate. The only evil then is weakness. Its symptoms
in the outer world must be met head-on, by force or by
craft. Did we really believe that this myth was dead?

Yet there was surprise in the 1920s when German
youth took to the roads of Europe as followers of the god
with rucksack and lute, even though they did not recognize what they were doing. People were even mildly
shocked when these young people celebrated the return
of Wotan with bloody sacrifices. Nietzsche, and even
others, had tried to speak of what was happening. But
Nietzsche's "Unknown God" (Wotan disguised as Diony-
sius) drove him mad, and for the most part only those who
were already possessed by the spirit of Wotan were willing
to listen. After all, the early Christian missionaries had
chopped down the trees sacred to the god, and believed
they could show that there was no place for these "created
gods" to come from except from the creation of men.[6]
People therefore believed that there was nothing to fear
from a myth.

But as Germany began to echo with the rhythm of the

military goose-step, it was apparent that something was happening. In 1936 Carl Jung, the Swiss psychiatrist, wrote the first of his deeply perceptive essays analyzing the catastrophes of Naziism, and later of World War II. He suggested that Wotan, as a metaphysical entity firmly seated in the German psyche, was a better explanation of the events than all the human reasoning about economic, political and psychological causes. He wrote that Wotan is a seizer or possessor of men, and

> ... unless one wishes to deify Hitler—which has indeed actually happened—[Wotan] is really the only explanation. . . . The impressive thing about the German phenomenon is that one man, who is obviously "possessed," has infected a whole nation to such an extent that everything is set in motion and has started rolling on its course towards perdition.[7]

Jung had a ringside seat in Switzerland as the rivers of blood flowed all around him. He was also aware, because of events in his personal life. Almost twenty years before Hitler was heard of, Jung had seen in a dream that there was a Siegfried, a warrior of Wotan, within himself. In the dream he had had to slay this figure, and he realized painfully that for him this was a Lucifer-angel of light which he had to put off. Siegfried (and Wotan) represented being dominated by "the will to power" which might have destroyed him. This kind of power usually leads to destruction, as Teutonic mythology reveals. These myths, as any fan of Wagner knows, usually end in disaster and the death and submergence of the gods themselves. When the going gets tough, Wotan does not wait around to be dealt with and be forced to mature.

Yet this myth of Wotan, or Lucifer as the earlier Christians realized, is still being played out on Main Street in our home towns, and this year in Washington, D.C., as well as during other past years. The Nazis were only more consistent and efficient in putting it to work. There are even those who worship Satan openly to gain this power, even if it does destroy. Those who believe in this myth, which suggests that anything evil can be turned to good if men will only become strong and clever enough, would do well to read Charles Williams' classic story of devotion to this power in his novel *Shadows of Ecstasy,* or C. S. Lewis' novel, *That Hideous Strength.* They are almost the equal of Goethe's *Faust,* and much easier reading for most moderns.

Jahweh and Evil

Behind the Christian understanding, there is another —of course very different—myth of a God of ultimate power. This is the Jahweh of the Old Testament, who was also adopted into Islam as the God Allah. But stop a moment. How can that be? Isn't this the same God that we Christians are all trying to find, the God who said, "You shall not have other gods besides me"? No, we Christians need to look carefully at the ancient idea of Jahweh usually depicted in the Old Testament, and realize that this is basically different from the God revealed by Jesus.

The older view pictures a God who is capricious or fickle and depends upon law; the other view pictures one who is steadfast and brings grace. One takes action for reasons of justice, the other out of love. One sends sickness; the other brings healing. One stands by the *lex talonis,* the rule of an eye for an eye and a tooth for a tooth; the other stands for forgiveness. And Allah is much like Jahweh. Both Jahweh and Allah are reactions against the amorality of the mother goddess, and against the multiplicity of gods which man can use to make any action seem right. Each stands as the sole God far above the universe, one God, single and alone. Each over-emphasizes the idea of monotheism to the exclusion of other independent spiritual realities.

This practically eliminates the idea of an evil force in the universe. To admit a real force of evil separate from God would weaken his stand against the amorality of nature, and so both Allah and Jahweh are forced to incorporate the very evil they wish to stand against. The result is that these Gods act like human beings. When they react against something, they incorporate it into themselves. They then have to avoid the problem of evil, unless they want to raise doubts about their own being. As Dante concludes when he is struggling with this problem in Paradise, God is just, and therefore when he wills something, it is right. If one is righteous and follows this God, he will be rewarded in this life and in the next.

There have been many protests against this point of view. It is not blasphemy to question it and face the facts. The world we live in is *not* just. Men often do their best and still are struck down by evil. In fact, one of the great things about the Old Testament is that it preserves this idea of God, and goes right on to incorporate the protest against it. In the Book of Job we find a righteous man crying out to God that he has suffered unjustly. Job did not mince words; he spoke his mind out of anger and pain, and God listened, and he finally acted. The result was that God came himself in human form to bring men the answer to Job's accusation.

As C. G. Jung has put it, God saw that he needed to manifest something more than law and justice and power. Jung's understanding came out of his own experience with suffering. It was expressed in a book which he called *The Answer to Job,* written within weeks after living through three pulmonary thromboses following a badly broken leg. This was Jung's own outcry to God, his realization that the insights of the Book of Job made necessary the coming of the Christ. And as the Christian myth reveals, God did understand, and came among men to confront the evil and give them rest from its relentless, nagging power. The myth of the dying and rising god, as we shall see, was still another attempt to deal with the problem of evil, which was rejected by the early Hebrew thinkers.

The "Knowing Ones" and Evil

And then there is the myth of special mystical knowledge given to a select few which is called Gnosticism. The Gnostics were a real threat to Christianity in early times, and their view is still quietly at work. It can be stated quite simply: all evil is concentrated in matter, and spirit is entirely good. The myths told of an original heaven, or pleroma, which once contained all spiritual reality, flowing together in perfection. Everything there moved in bliss and harmony and this would have remained for all time if there had not been a cosmic catastrophe.

This swirling mass of pure spirituality blew apart, and some of the fragments of spirit drifted down into the chaos below, into the evil darkness where matter clashed and collided. As a result, out of the formless, resistant matter, the earth was created, and the fragments of spirit were lodged in it and developed into men. Far above the earth some of the original heaven still remained, and in between there were layers of spiritual reality left by the cosmic explosion, each larger and more perfect than the one below. The pinpoints of spirit in man aspired to leave the evil world, to rise and somehow get back to the original pleroma.

No one knows for sure where these ideas began. There seem to have been traces of them in Greek thinking by the fifth century B. C., and later on in Plato (which for some people spoils Plato's otherwise incomparable view of reality). But by the time Christianity was in full swing, some of the better thinkers of the ancient world had become involved in the mystical practices of this system, and were busy trying to change Christianity into a Gnostic system. What they offered was a completely different way of salvation, based on a contradictory view of evil.

Since to the Gnostic the sole destructive evil was matter itself, the goal was to separate man's soul from the earth, so that it could rise naturally towards the pleroma, or heaven. And the way of doing this was by knowledge, or *gnosis*. By elaborate steps the individual was led to know the nature of reality and the stages through which he would pass, entering the lower heavens and finally ascending to perfect freedom. This was accompanied by ascetic practices which had a double purpose. They made sure the individual knew he was trapped in the immediate world and that there was nothing good about it. But the worst sin was not just to remain caught in matter. It was to be caught by sexuality, because the result was conception and new life, which simply meant that another valuable bit of spirit became stuck and had to be rescued from matter.

Thus sex became the cardinal sin, and chastity the prime virtue, essentially denying the idea of a body valuable enough to heal or to be resurrected. This religious attitude was strong in the Roman world, and even Augustine was attracted to the Manichean sect and spent nine years trying to accept what they said. A great deal later we find this same point of view expressed all over again in Christian circles. It hit both Protestants and Catholics at the same time in Puritanism and Jansenism.

None of these myths of evil and salvation from it, is exactly dead in our Christian world. And unless we know something about them, and about our own mythological heritage, it is very difficult to tell which belief we are acting on. How can we even tell whether Christianity is

· our choice or not unless we know what it offers in contrast to other myths? Let us begin now to compare our own mythological heritage with these other points of view.

The Ideas of Zoroaster

In our own religious heritage, one of the great contributions was the mythological understanding of evil offered by Zoroaster (or Zarathustra) about the beginning of the sixth century B.C. Zoroaster grew up in the land of Persia, with an experience of religion much like shamanism. Out of these incomplete and rather naive experiences, he fused the monumental system that bore his name. About the time that Persia was becoming a world power, it became the state religion of that country, whose influence lasted until the Arab conquest in the sixth century of our own era. But long before Christ, the influence of Zoroaster was spread across the great empire of Alexander. In its very beginnings Western thought was touched and fertilized by the ideas of Zoroastrianism.

The basis of that religion was Zoroaster's view of one supreme god, Ahura Mazda, from whom all creation flowed, and his twin sons who were given the original choice between good and evil. At the end of this first creation, the followers of the son who had chosen truth, justice, and light would share in a new creation. But those who followed the evil son, who had chosen destruction, would be purged. But gradually Ahura Mazda became identified with his good son. A more elaborate myth grew up which told that the evil one, Ahriman, had existed from the beginning alongside of the one, otherwise all-powerful god.

It told of an initial struggle, from which Ahriman fell back into the dark abyss for a time, while Ahura Mazda (or Ormazd) created a realm of spiritual beings, and then a corresponding material world. He gave the souls of men a choice of remaining undeveloped spirits, or of becoming incarnate in the physical world and helping to fight Ahriman. They chose to be born and to struggle with evil. Ahriman then entered the physical world with his demons and his creation. But there he was trapped by the forces of good, and the way was opened for Zoroaster to bring religion to men. Three times a new savior would come, until finally the third would dispense judgment and usher in a new world in which finite time would merge with infinite time, and mortals who had struggled against evil would become immortal.

The reason for following Ahura Mazda was faith in this eventual outcome, and this was a faith that the real power lay in the hands of his spiritual creation. Good and evil were both seen as spiritual realities, which have a direct influence on matter and the physical world, as well as on men's psyches and spirits. And so those who remained faithful to the good in life, to truth, light and justice, could expect results in three ways.

These followers of Ahura Mazda would ultimately share in the realm that belonged to him and in his final defeat of evil. And so, second, in the here and now they could also turn to his powers of light for help in dealing with troubles like illness or natural disasters, which seem to result from some malevolent force in the world. And third, through their moral action and religious practice, men could depend on Ahura Mazda to awaken more of their own human power to resist evil and work towards defeating it in the present world. Because of the mythological division between the forces of light and those of darkness, men were able to confront these opposites of good and evil and begin to deal with them directly.

It is doubtful whether men can really come to grips with the problem of evil, either intellectually or morally, until it has been stated in some such way mythologically.

Moral action stems from such a division; the very energy to act consistently springs from a belief that such action may be worthwhile. The myth of Ahura Mazda provided a statement of the problem, and a belief that men would gain by facing it morally, neither striking out at random nor just taking things as they come. It is almost impossible to put too much stress on the influence of this primary understanding of evil. As this point of view interacted with the ideas of Greece and the Near East, it left its impact upon all of the religions which are a part of our heritage today. Specifically, it provided the soil in which the ideas of Judaism were growing in the century just before the birth of the Christ.

It also left a remnant who still show the effect of that religious belief. The few thousand "Gabars" who remain in Iran and the "Parsees" in Bombay and other places in India and Pakistan are still known for their industry and prosperity in spite of the difficulties of persecution and migration to a strange, absorbing land. As one writer has noted, this religion has left its "mark in the dignified bearing and peaceableness characteristic of this ancient, good-living and thrifty people."[8] For them the name Ahura Mazda speaks of the sacred fire which is still used in their worship of light and goodness. Strange, but for most of us in my generation it means a brand of light bulbs,[9] and now a new kind of automotive power.

Still, as important as this religious attitude has been, there was a problem with it. The real victory over evil was to be all in the future. There was little to suggest that the divine struggle, the bout between Ahura Mazda and Ahriman, would have a direct, ringside effect on the individual and his own defeat of evil. Perhaps this was one reason that Zoroastrianism died out except for a remnant who keep their way of life closely guarded against the practical, down-to-earth ideas of Islam which displaced it.

On the other hand, the myth of the dying and rising

god did hold out hope to people in their own struggle with evil. Through ritual and symbol, and finally in the actual events of history, it offered men participation with the god in his defeat and in his victory and new life. Let's now return to this myth of the dying and rising god, and to the Hebrew religion which grew up in the land where that myth was strong. We shall see how these two myths, of Ahura Mazda-Ahriman and the dying and rising god, met and merged.

IV

The Dying
and Rising God

Christianity is based on the account of a man, Jesus of Nazareth, who died and rose again from the dead. According to the New Testament, the followers of this man met with him after his death and shared in his new life and power. Because of what he did and said during his life, and particularly because of his resurrection, they saw him as an incarnation of God, who met evil, defeated it in dying and rising again, and gave his Spirit to his followers, transforming them. Over the centuries these experiences of encounter and transformation were described, and an understanding was worked out which was finally expressed by the idea of the Trinity. And out of those encounters came the understanding, not that Jesus is like God, but that God is like Jesus, for through him we get a real picture of God, face to face.

For many centuries the basic idea of Jesus as the God who died and rose again was central to the Christian faith. But once the world view of the Middle Ages was seriously questioned, men began to wonder about the idea of a dying and rising God. It made little sense to rational thinkers who were coming to see the world as an orderly mechanism run by physical laws. If God existed at all, he was the creator of invariable laws, laws which could not change, and so the resurrection appeared to be a capricious breaking of law, if not an outright impossibility.

Besides that, it began to appear that there was nothing unique about the Christian story of a dying and rising god. Studies of mythology, particularly James Frazer's *Golden Bough,* pointed out that there had been several such myths right in the area where Christianity began, with obvious similarities to the Christian story. To many intellectuals this meant that the New Testament account was simply one more of these fanciful tales, on which men had based a childish attempt to influence nature and control the sun or the weather or the growth of plants.

The ancient peoples seem to have had quite a different understanding of these myths, which is also shared by many modern thinkers, and we need to look more closely at their meaning for that world in which Christianity was developing.

Understanding an Ancient Myth

As fabulous and strange as these tales may seem to us, they are scarcely simple stories. The theme of death and renewal that runs through them does suggest the cycles of nature, sometimes very specifically. But there was also a commentary on human behavior running through them which was probably responsible for the rites and celebrations that grew up around these myths in sophisticated centers like Rome and Athens. Even so, it may seem foolish to go into detail about them. But since they have often been used to make fun of the Christian story, and since there *are* parallels, as well as differences, let us see what the stories did express.

Perhaps the most familiar of them is the myth of Adonis and Aphrodite,* whose rites were celebrated in places all the way from Athens to Alexandria. This myth has also been a theme for artists and poets, including

---

*Or Venus and Adonis in the Roman version.

Shakespeare, in various periods. The story starts with incestuous love, sparked of course by the goddess herself, who is thus responsible for the extraordinary birth of Adonis. His mother was about to be killed when the gods took pity and turned her into a tree. A child then burst forth from its trunk who was so beautiful that Aphrodite immediately loved him. She hid him in a box and sent him to the underworld to be cared for secretly. But there he captivated even the powers of death, and when the time came for his return, they refused to let him go. Aphrodite had to appeal to Zeus and accept a compromise. She could bring Adonis back to earth, but a part of each year he had to return to the underworld.

A second version of the story then tells that Aphrodite loved the youth so much that she tried to be with him all the time, even on the hunts which he loved. She begged him not to hunt beasts that kill, but he would not listen and one day a wounded boar turned on Adonis and gored him. Aphrodite heard his moans from far off and rushed to the spot to find him lying dead in a pool of blood. Weeping, she gathered his blood and mixed it with sweet substance so that wherever a drop fell, crimson flowers would spring up fresh each year.

The story of Tammuz and Ishtar starts on a more earthy note, and its theme was not elaborated, possibly because the cuneiform alphabet (used in the ancient Middle East where they were worshiped) did not encourage lengthy descriptions. Ishtar (or Innana) chose Tammuz for her husband because his flocks were fat and their milk was good. He became guardian of a city. And one day he sat on his throne in robes of state and did not rise to greet the goddess. She flew into a rage and ordered demons to carry him off to the underworld (in another reference, she "bruised his wing"). Ishtar then made a perilous descent into the underworld, and Tammuz was sent back to her rejoicing. Later he was spoken of as the Lord of the underworld who controlled the demons that cause sickness, and the wailing for him was even mentioned in the Old Testament.[1]

Attis, on the other hand, was worshiped in Rome almost as long as the empire lasted, and the tales about him multiplied. Here again was the story of a beautiful youth who was loved. In one version the love was homosexual, in another it was pure love to which Attis was unfaithful, and in a third it was incestuous. In each case he was driven to madness and castrated himself and died. His resurrection was symbolized in various stories by his being changed into a pine tree, or by violets which sprang up from his blood. The worship of Attis began in the Near East, where it grew up along with that of Cybele, who was known as the great mother of the gods.

Finally, there was the myth of Osiris on which much of the Hellenistic mystery religion was based. One of these temples which can still be seen is the temple of Isis in Pompeii. Osiris, the Egyptian king who was young and "fair of face," was loved deeply by his sister-wife, the great goddess Isis. Together, it was told, they turned Egypt from a land of savages into a settled agricultural nation. But their brother Set was jealous and murdered Osiris, finally tearing his body to pieces. In the end it was recovered by Isis and restored to life. Like Tammuz, Osiris then became known as the ruler of the dead. Plutarch, who became an initiate of Osirian mysteries, wrote of giving up bodily passions to find a "pure and unseen realm" as a follower of Osiris.

Each one of these myths, and the forms of worship that came from them, spoke of the cycles of nature, of the death or dormancy of vegetation in the dark days of winter, and the bursting forth of new life in the spring. The major celebrations usually took place in springtime, at about the time of our Easter, and often sacrifices were offered when the fields were planted. In Egypt earth and seeds were mixed to form tiny statues of Osiris that were planted with the rest of the seeds to insure their fertility, while in Rome the festival of Attis and Cybele began with the sacrifice of a six-year-old bull. The world of nature had undoubtedly given man his first cogent reasons for seeking some kind of help outside himself, and it continued to feed his rituals, as well as his life.

Yet even the most primitive of these peoples realized that their myths had more meaning than that. The people of that time had a deep sense of need for the divine in human life, and an understanding of symbolism. It has taken modern mechanized man to conceive of the idea that matter means matter and nothing else, and that once it is established that a ritual was needed at the time of planting or harvesting, this is a fact that can have no other meaning. But a real sense of the divine teaches that nature itself is the symbol of the struggle with spiritual powers, rather than the other way around. The natural elements in these myths spoke to people of a deeper reality, as men like Plutarch and some of the philosophers brought out. These elements spoke of destructive forces, forces of death in man's life, and they also suggest that there is another force which can be victorious in the end, bringing a change like the change from winter to spring. Nature's rebirth itself speaks to men as a symbol of their own rising to a new birth of consciousness and spirit.

These myths, then, offer graphic descriptions of man's struggle with darkness and death, or—in less colorful words —with unconsciousness and destructive evil. They start in each case by defining some result of that evil, such as jealousy, or unreasoning pride, or love that overwhelms and restricts. They then frame this in the perspective of a human death, and show that a positive spiritual power (the goddess herself in some cases, or the ruler of the gods in others) can be enlisted through sorrow to bring the dead one back from burial in the underworld. In two instances the restored individual is then seen as having the ability to deal with the powers of the underworld and control them. He can even control death itself.

Around each of these stories religious celebrations grew up which gave people a chance to act out elements of this struggle (or to watch the drama acted out), and thus to experience the emotions aroused by it. As men have realized today who are studying human problems, myths often speak quite clearly of forces which affect individuals adversely, which cannot be controlled just by conscious will. Through their rituals these myths of Adonis and Attis, of Tammuz and Osiris, allowed men to identify with the god in his struggle with such forces of evil, to share in his defeat and death, and then to have a part in the victory of his resurrection and new life.

The Worship of Adonis and Attis

The rituals symbolizing the death and resurrection of Adonis and his several counterparts were deeply moving. The best descriptions of them come from the celebrations of Attis in Rome, and also the rites of Adonis in Alexandria. Here in the springtime effigies of Adonis and Aphrodite were laid side by side, surrounded by flowers and fruit as if for a marriage. Then with all the feeling of a funeral, crowds of weeping mourners, many of them women with loosened hair and bare breasts, carried the image of the dead god to the shore and committed it to the sea. The crowds participating in grief remind one of the actual funerals of Lincoln and Kennedy. But almost at the same moment, the mourners began to sing of how Adonis would return to them.

In Phoenicia, when the rivers ran red with clay from the mountains like the blood of Adonis, the believers mourned his death on one day and celebrated his resurrection the next. The weeping and wailing for him in Athens were recorded before one of the great battles, when the troops had to march off through the lament, and in Antioch even in Christian times it was told how the Emperor Julian had first come there during the rites.

Two hundred years before Christ the worship of Attis was becoming popular in Rome, and as might be expected the Romans put order into the worship. For nearly two weeks the processions and sacrifices occupied people. A pine tree, which was sacred to Attis, was carried through the streets and placed in the cave of Cybele, the mother-goddess, to show her sorrow for having allowed his self-mutilation and death to happen; or in some places a great beam wound with cloth was used. Then a day of abstinence began, and people gathered to wail and watch a wild ceremony at the temple. As drums and cymbals played, the priests lacerated their bodies, and the neophytes castrated themselves symbolically (or sometimes in reality) to become like Attis. Finally the days of rejoicing came, and there were equal demonstrations of joy for the god's return.

Using various symbols, the story of each of these gods was acted out to express essentially the same thing.* Each one expresses the need of the individual to separate out from some dark, instinctual force which reaches out for human beings and pulls them destructively into inertia. There was a monster, the ancestor of the youth who desired him, or a boar that gored him, or the hold of the underworld itself. In each case the great mother goddess (or the goddess of love) was involved, symbolizing the dark earth, the unconscious womb of reality out of which all things emerge, both good and evil.

Each year the young god was believed to die and rise

---

*The Osirian mysteries were largely secret and thus we do not have complete descriptions of them; we have mentioned one of the reasons why the rites of Tammuz were not better described.

again, rescuing men from the bondage of darkness and evil. It was understood that as the believer suffered with the god, life was reborn; there was hope; and evil and darkness were defeated. His inner discouragement and depression, his anxiety and terror were overcome. It was magnificent psychotherapy and more.

Yet it was beyond the capacity of men at that time to imagine that this could happen once to an actual human being, and thus become sufficient for all men for all time. They could not see that the only way this action could be taken out of its unfinished cycle of mythological timelessness was for it to happen in time and history. History was not yet that real to them. The inner world was the one which really mattered.

Adonis and Jahweh

Among the Hebrews, however, this idea would take shape. And here we find a new kind of God. The Jewish God, Jahweh, has turned his back upon the darkness of primeval chaos, the unconscious matrix of the great mother. Mythologically, he is Adonis or Attis in a reaction formation. He is like an adolescent standing against his mother, without realizing that one is just as tied to the mother when he is reacting against her as when he is being overly obedient. It is an interesting sidelight that the usual alternative for the divine name Yahweh, as it became too sacred to utter in public, was "Adonai," or "my Lord." God was simply called by the Semitic equivalent for the Greek word Adonis.

Early Jewish religion, then, represents a second stage of religious development in which the masculine stands out against the all-encompassing feminine, which is seen as unalterably dark and destructive because it contains and does not let the individual go. Ishtar, Astarte, Cybele,

Isis, Aphrodite—Jahweh stands against them all. How violently the Hebrew prophets denounce anything pertaining to the queen of heaven, the abominations and harlotry, the women wailing for Tammuz, the idolatries of Baal—many of these practices probably very much like the celebrations of Attis and Adonis. How defensive the early Israelites are in the land in which Cybele and Ishtar are ruling deities; they protest too much.

Yet there are certain other connections between Jahweh and Adonis. The Hebraic prohibition against eating pork is reminiscent of the same ritual behavior among the followers of Adonis. These believers, of course, would not eat the flesh of the boar or pig because that animal was responsible for the death of their lord. It is also quite possible that the religious practice of circumcision represents a symbolic castration, a modification of the rite related to the great mother, and almost certainly a reaction to sexual relations on her terms.

Jahweh does not even have room for the warmth and understanding of the mother goddess, let alone her amoral vagaries. He has become all justice and strength and power and consciousness (when he is not overtaken by one of his more punitive moods). Probably this reaction of masculine power against the instinctive, earthy side of life—the dark earth mother—is necessary in the development of human consciousness and man's power to work with himself and his environment. It is undoubtedly a stage that men have to go through if they are to discriminate between good and evil and realize that they can have the power to choose between them. In many ways Islam appears to be a return to the masculine God of the Old Testament, a God the desert nomads needed in their struggle for consciousness and self-determination.

Perhaps there are some of us who really believe that separating oneself out from the all-encompassing "mother" is no longer a problem for men and women today, that they should have no trouble growing up and making their own moral decisions. If so, one needs to talk with some of today's college students of both sexes. Or, one may be able to learn something about our moral dilemma by listening to his own dreams. The symbols and the pull of the great mother goddesses are still quite alive in the depth of the human psyche. Recently two significant dreams have been told to me which illustrate the reality of the problem quite clearly.

The first dream, which centered around the figure of a boar, came to an unsuspecting man in his mid-thirties who had a real problem relating to the dark "mother," although he had not realized it. In the dream he saw himself getting up from the dining table to perform some habitual action. As he did, he glanced up to a shelf on the opposite wall to see the stuffed head of a wild boar sitting on it. He was staring at it when the animal suddenly gave him a broad wink. This man found it easier to be controlled by the "mother" than to relate to her and carry his own responsibility. The dream and the almost indecent wink shocked him into realizing the darkness and evil he was facing. Seeing the experience in terms of the Adonis myth, he suddenly saw his own problem very clearly. In the other instance, a graduate student dreamed of a dark, demonic woman who came into his room, ripped his heart out of his body, and stood squeezing it in her hand. Images like these are anything but extinct today. They occur among the most sophisticated of us, especially among the highly intellectual persons who have cut themselves off from their earthy darkness and deny its existence.

The Dying and Rising God in History

In Christianity—and also in a different form in later Judaism—we find a further stage of development. Here the spirit of Jahweh, or the Lord, comes into creative contact with the woman Mary. Mary is of the earth; she is feminine, compassionate, a caring and an obedient person. In fact, she is a purified and humanized form of the great mother. Out of this union of the masculine, just and powerful Jahweh and the warm, loving and accepting Mary there is born the Christ who is both God and man. In Christ, mythologically understood, the stream of the great mother goddesses is joined and mingled with that of Hebraic religion and Jahweh. What had been opposed is now reunited. The opposites come together creatively, and there is resolution and wholeness.

From the point of view of man, the impregnation of Mary is also the myth of the soul of man, the symbol of a union between the masculine and feminine sides of a man's personality. This means a new development of one's inner masculinity, which impregnates his feminine side, bringing a new realization and appreciation of these qualities within him. This union of the opposites within a man takes place so that a new and creative life, the Christ life, may be born in man, superseding, transcending, and transforming both the masculine ego and the feminine unconsciousness which have given it birth. The development within a woman appears to be parallel, since the consciousness which is involved is essentially a masculine quality. This is the myth of human development, the myth of the hero who is thus able to confront and conquer darkness and evil. It speaks of the reality of the spiritual world in which man participates.

This historical Christ, who was born of the actual prototype of this union, suffered and died and rose again. But with Christ it was done once and for all. Since the myth was acted out in history, there was no need for it to be repeated in spiritual reality as the older myths of the dying god were repeated each year. It had happened once and for all, and men could share in it in the Mass. Those who let the mythological pattern set by Christ become an essential part of their lives also share in his victory and his power over evil and death. In a later chapter we shall suggest some of the ways in which we can participate in this victory.

As we go on to consider the actual life of Jesus of Nazareth, we shall also see how he accepted and used the third myth of Zoroastrianism and its approach to evil. This understanding of evil was already coming into acceptance in writings like the Book of Tobit and also in other Hebrew thinking of that time. It provided an approach completely different from either the moral indignation of Jahweh or the feeling and emotional reaction of the dying and rising gods. By accepting and using the Zoroastrian idea of Satan and demons as responsible for evil, Jesus offered the understanding which helps men to combine and temper the earthy feminine elements of the great mother religions with the masculine and moral consciousness of Jahweh.

Of course one can point out innumerable parallels drawn by Frazer and others between the Christian myth and rituals and those of the other myths and rites of the dying and rising gods. These parallels, however, are no problem for the sophisticated Christian who sees the older myths as imaginative, visionary representations of spiritual truths and realities. The followers of these gods seldom suggested that they existed or were experienced in any way but spiritually. But then the pattern itself at last broke into history in the life of Jesus of Nazareth.

Because men had dreamed of such events and had told the stories of them that are called myths does not make the Christian story any less plausible, but actually far more so. Once the myth is understood, not as a human invention, but as a pattern of the structure of reality, then one would expect to find such patterns emerging in men's dreams and visions and imagination before they become realized in history. Someone had to be made ready for an actual event of this kind so that its momentous nature did not escape his attention when it did occur. The understanding that these myths prefigured the reality which broke through in Jesus of Nazareth makes real sense—unless one is convinced of being caught in a materialistic world, isolated from any other reality.

In fact it worries many Christian thinkers far more to realize how completely we have come to ignore the mythological and myth-making character of the life of Jesus. This is particularly true of those Christian thinkers who speak out of their experience rather than out of their rational ideas. Those who have dealt with their own inner darkness and chaos, and have tried to help others to find a firmer footing within themselves, know that man does not move out into the world without his myths. They realize that he needs this myth in particular, and that it is rather difficult to find its reality within oneself when the basic stories of myths are considered fictional and untrue to begin with.

Rational theology simply hamstrings God for most people. By denying the usefulness of these forms—the imaginative, the mythological, the spiritual, and most of the ways they break into a human life—we finally depotentiate God in our lives almost entirely. As one Scottish theologian with his own touch of humor has put it, "Religion is necessarily mythological in character. . . . The attempt to divest the figure of Jesus Christ of such modes of presentation rests upon the assumption that . . . [they] are an essential handicap. But is this not exactly parallel to saying that Jesus' body was a handicap, and does not this in turn imperil the reality of the incarnation?"[2] We would do well to ask ourselves: What *did* make that baby born on a desert ridge in Palestine two thousand years ago so important that he still affects the lives of quite a few of us?

When myth is understood as a revealer of spiritual

reality at work in man's unconscious psyche (or soul), then the Christian story can become as alive and vital as it was in the beginning. In much the same way as then, it can bring a living connection with the very depth of the most real of all reality—the reality of spirit which has more than a little to do with God. It can also bring the individual his own victory over the dark forces of destruction, and this has very practical implications for living out one's existence in this tense and anxious world.

If this is so, it is rather important for us to realize it from a practical Christian point of view, for it is difficult to find a celebration of the rites of Attis and Cybele, or a sacrifice of Adonis, to share in today. On the other hand, the Christian myth is still very much around even yet. In spite of the efforts of several theologians and churches to "demythologize" it, the Christian story is at hand, particularly in the Christian Mass, waiting to meet the individual and transform and revitalize him. The Mass can not only offer the individual a vital mythological and spiritual encounter today, but its reality is there even when those who celebrate it do not understand what they are doing.

The question of the reality of myth can never be settled by reason alone. Basically it is only experience which can reveal whether the myth of the dying and rising god represents a possible conquest of death and evil, or whether it rests solely on the cycles of vegetation and man's understanding of them. Does this myth still emerge in the hearts and dreams of men? Do men still find transformation when they encounter the reality and power of the myth? Or is all this just wishful thinking, an illusory wish-fulfillment? Actually the answer can only be given by those who have dealt with human darkness, depression, and evil, and have seen the effect of the Easter message in transforming men. And myths do have some very important evidence to offer modern man about the nature of the universe, both physical and spiritual. Let's turn to this evidence, starting with a brief look at the story of Jesus to refresh our minds and imagination about the details of this story which has been such an integral part of our civilization from its most vital period on through. We shall leave much, of course, for each reader to investigate on his own.

V
Jesus
of Nazareth

During the reign of Tiberius, when Pontius Pilate was governor of Judea, a new prophet suddenly appeared in that small, far-off corner of the Roman Empire. The man was unknown outside of his own town of Nazareth—until he began to gather great crowds wherever he went, and to antagonize the religious leaders of the Jews. He proclaimed a new message, the good news that the kingdom of God was at hand, right around the corner, and those who were sensitive to such things could feel its power and reality. Many of them were poor or sick people who were caught in a religion of laws and had felt that there was no one who cared about their situation, and nothing could be done about it, until they were touched by this man who was called Jesus.

The God whose kingdom he proclaimed could be addressed as "Abba," which is a familiar name more like "papa" or "daddy" than "Father." He was not like the harsh and distant God of so much of the Old Testament. None of the prophets that were known from the scriptures had spoken so easily and in such a familiar way about God. In fact, the whole message of this Jesus was so astounding that it was a wonder anyone believed it at all. He told of a God who was offering to take people into his kingdom right away, a God who is as loving as a tender father with a small child.

We have heard so much about this teaching of love that we have become immunized against it. We scarcely notice how radical and strange it is. Just try to imagine what it actually means: If this love is at the heart and center of reality, the love of a tender father for his small child, how are we to follow such a God? If we believe this, won't we try to show it by acting in the same way? Jesus taught that God wants to share the best he has with men. Those who are really looking for God's kingdom do not have to wait for the end of the age, or until they are dead. Its life and power can be experienced right now, in this life. As Jesus explained, that kingdom can come on earth, as in heaven. And the reason people believed him was that he brought an experience of it and taught them to take this experience to others.

He also taught that men are caught between two worlds. There was the physical world which he knew and appreciated well, as his exquisite parables often reveal. But he taught that there was also another world, a spiritual world which impinged directly upon men and was as important, no, more important than the physical one, because here the kingdom of God was found, as well as forces of evil with which men needed help. Jesus suggested that his followers conclude their praying by asking to be delivered from "the Evil One" (for this is an accurate translation of the Greek words of the Lord's Prayer) . The important thing was that men now had a chance to win out in their constant battle with evil. The kingdom of God was closer than they had thought, and its power was able to put to flight the forces of this Evil One, the dark and demonic forces which reach out for man from the spiritual world and apparently seek to destroy him.

As Jesus showed, partly in action and partly in words, evil attacks men in three ways. Morally it brings them under the domination of self-centeredness and pettiness, of hatred and violence, thus taking over their wills. The

power of the coming kingdom released men from this
domination through repentance and forgiveness. Mental
illness was a second way in which the forces of evil possess
men, distracting and dominating their minds completely.
In the new kingdom these demonic forces could be dealt
with directly and compelled to let go of their hold on men,
thus bringing release from demon possession or mental
illness.

Finally, Jesus considered that physical illness, rather
than being the result of God's anger with men and his
need to punish them, is actually due to the corrupting
action of evil. This is the third effort of the Evil One to
dominate men, by destroying their bodies as well as their
wills and minds. One of the main signs of the approaching
kingdom which was expressed by Jesus of Nazareth was his
power to heal. It was one of the most significant characteristics of his whole ministry, as I have shown in some detail
in my book *Healing and Christianity*. Yet modern Christianity has largely ignored this amazing ministry, dismiss-
ing it either as mythological fiction or as something that
is simply no longer important in modern times. In so
doing, it has discarded one of the main expressions of
God's love revealed in the Gospels. Anyone who has been
really sick will certainly recognize how thoroughly love is
expressed by healing, by whatever means.

Besides these ways in which Jesus touched men through
experiences of the kingdom of God, he also drew them by
his remarkable ability to teach. He spoke with authority.
In fact, he spoke of the kingdom of God as one who knew
it from the inside and could vouch for the things he described. He put his message simply in images and stories
that were easy to remember, making fresh, even startling
comparisons that held people's attention. He compared
God and the kingdom of heaven with a woman who swept
the whole house to find a single lost coin, with the return
of a prodigal son who still sounds so familiar today that

we might think of a "hippie," with finding buried treasure in a field, with being tossed out of a party for not wearing the right clothes (a wedding garment), or with a farmer who told his workers not to bother with the weeds because they would probably make a mistake and pull up his wheat at the same time.

In dozens of such images—homely and understandable, yet with a new twist—Jesus brought home to men the reality of a loving God who wishes to reach through into men's hearts and lives and rescue them from the power and domination of evil. Over and over he pointed out the many ways God has of guiding men on the path of growth, maturity and wholeness. As John Sanford shows so well in *The Kingdom Within,* there is a depth to these teachings that will probably never be exhausted. Furthermore, when Jesus spoke of a resurrected life beyond the grave, he did not picture a grey, meaningless existence like the Hebrew idea of "Sheol." He made men aware that there is a life to come that is worth working towards. He showed, in more ways than one, that it is a culmination of this present life, worth even the tragedy and agony of slavery in the Roman Empire.

The Life of Jesus

There was a time not too long ago when many Christians doubted that much could be known about the historical reality of Jesus of Nazareth. It had just dawned on many students how important the angels and demons, the healings and visions were in the life of Jesus. Since they had no place for such things, they came to believe that the story of his life was so mixed up with legend and fanciful ingredients that the two could hardly be separated. A naive understanding grew that much of the New Testament was based on the imagination of the early church, that many parts of it were inventions, created myths rather than myth lived by an actual man in history. As a result there was more guesswork about the origins of ideas in the record than there was study of the facts found in it.[1]

More recently, however, scholars have realized that the facts are there. They can be traced quite clearly in the Biblical record, and this has now been done in more than one careful study. In his book *Jesus of Nazareth,* Günther Bornkamm has recounted the history of Jesus' life in detail, while Norman Perrin at the University of Chicago has done the same thing for the message of Jesus in his work *Rediscovering the Teaching of Jesus.* It is evident that the data about Jesus of Nazareth, his life, his ministry, his death, his resurrection, came from history. There may be disagreement about some of the details, but essentially the best of modern studies of the gospels attest to the fact that the story told in the New Testament actually happened. If we find myth here, it was myth written in history, not just arising from the creative imagination of men.

In two of the gospels the life of Jesus begins with the story of Mary, the young virgin betrothed to Joseph. She is described as the perfectly obedient one, one who was willing to take the consequences of carrying a child of the Holy Spirit in spite of what her fiancé would say, in spite of the way women would gossip around the village well. There are dreams and the visitation of an angel, and then the long trip to Bethlehem for the Roman census. After the trek over rugged Palestinian roads, with only a donkey to make it easier, the couple are turned away from the inn. And Mary brings forth her special child in a stable under the rays of a great star. Shepherds who hear of it from angels, and wise men who follow the star, come to pay homage. Almost immediately the family is forced to flee into Egypt and stay there until after Herod's death.

From this point Jesus and his family disappear into the village life, except for one brief incident in the temple when Jesus was twelve years old. In all four gospels the story picks up when he is grown and John the Baptist comes out of the wilderness offering to baptize people. Jesus is baptized, and immediately there is a vision of the Holy Spirit, and he is forced to go into the wilderness by himself and be faced and tempted by the devil.

Although many scholars distrust this first part of the story of Jesus' life because of its mythological quality, I am inclined to believe that it represents the reality of history just because it is so full of mythological elements. I have known too many present-day experiences that were almost as mythological to dismiss these elements as unreal. At times of crisis and change, perfectly ordinary people, people I have known well, sometimes have the same kind of visions and extraordinary experiences that can only be described as new birth, or baptism, or temptation. If they can happen today, why not at the very time when God was breaking into the world as a human being? There is also the fact that the birth story in particular often touches people in crisis, bringing real illumination to them. One woman has told me, for instance, of a difficult childbirth when she received strength and comfort from simply knowing within herself the events surrounding Jesus' birth as Luke recorded them.

This part is only the beginning, however, and most modern scholars are in essential agreement about what happened after that. There are many mythological elements in the story which we do not try to include in this brief outline. Visions, angels and demons, prophecy, and other related experiences are important in the story. And of course there are scholars who try to eliminate these elements, although they reveal things that are extremely important for man's understanding of himself and his religion. But whether they came from racial memories, or from events surrounding one individual, is not the point. God may have chosen that particular race and prepared them by experiences like these to make the incarnation possible; or he may have picked Jesus and started him out in exactly that way; it doesn't really matter that much. What does matter is that God became man in a specific time in history. The fact that there was a man Jesus who lived as he did, and died and was resurrected, is certainly the most important part of the story.

When Jesus then appeared on the public scene, it was in Galilee, and he emerged almost like a comet sweeping over the Hebrew lands. For three years (more or less) he preached the good news of the coming kingdom of God, he taught about the way people could prepare in order to find that kingdom, and he healed. Everywhere that he went, Jesus healed. Even his enemies attested to this fact, but said that it was by Beelzebub or the prince of the devils that he healed. People flocked to hear him and to be healed by him.

Jesus gave men the Lord's prayer and his incomparable teaching in the Sermon on the Mount, but his greatest teaching was in parables which are still as fresh after two thousand years of retelling. Who can forget the father who stands looking out into the desert waiting for his profligate son to return home, his arms outstretched and ready to pour on him forgiveness, mercy, goodness, acceptance, love? And still the elder brother stands back judging. What a picture of God's incomprehensible love for man no matter what he is or has been.

The story of healing which still strikes me most deeply is a double one when Jesus was asked to go to the sick child of Jairus. As he passed through the press of the crowd, a woman who had been hemorrhaging a long time reached out and touched him and immediately was well. He knew that power had flowed out from him. And when he turned to the crowd asking who had touched him with purpose, she came forward to acknowledge what had happened. Then he came to the house of Jairus and, finding that the daughter was dead, he then raised the child from the dead and gave her back to her sorrowing parents.

This man seemed to have power over nature as well. After one of his crowded days among people, Jesus and his disciples retired to a ship and put off into the Sea of Galilee. He lay down in the prow of the ship and fell fast asleep. A storm arose and the disciples feared that the ship would founder; and so they woke up Jesus who rebuked the wind, and the waves calmed and they were safe. Then he admonished his disciples for having so little faith. There is a similar story in the life of a Navajo medicine man told by Franc Newcomb in her book, *Hosteen Klah*. Shamans seem to have power over nature as well as over man, and Jesus was the greatest of all shamans, the archetypal shaman. One reason so few people understand Jesus of Nazareth or the New Testament is that they put Jesus into the role of a Greek lecturer on ethics and morality, whereas he was really a shaman, a healer and saver of men.

One by one he selected a group of twelve disciples from every walk of life, men who gave up everything to follow him. They were commissioned to have a ministry similar to his. This was the original community, the foretaste of the kingdom, and around them was another larger group of disciples. These men preached, taught, cast out demons, and healed. Even women were welcomed into the fellowship, and Jesus treated them with more respect than almost any other leader, religious or otherwise, to this time.

At the same time he condemned the religious leaders in Judea, both the Pharisees and the priestly party, for their neglect of the poor and those who were outcasts. Jesus welcomed sinners and the poor into his fellowship. He did not hesitate to break the sabbath laws to heal, or to show in other ways that "the sabbath was made for man, not man for the sabbath." He said out and out that the authorities enjoyed imposing the law as a whole on others instead of examining their own response to it. Gradually he gained the enmity not only of the official religious leaders, but of the government as well. He told a would-be follower, "Foxes have holes, and birds have nests; but the son of man has nowhere to lay his head." For a time Jesus and his disciples even withdrew into Phoenicia, between Tyre and Sidon.

Soon after returning from his self-imposed exile, Jesus began to explain in more detail to his disciples what lay ahead. Just before the Passover they started back to Jerusalem. He knew full well the reception he would receive from the authorities. When the holy city was filling up for the feast, Jesus made a triumphal entry, riding a colt he had sent for by clairvoyant insight. He came as a prophet, surrounded by crowds looking for the Messiah to deliver them. He went directly to the temple and threw down the gauntlet to the officials. Driving out the monychangers and buyers and sellers who were set up to promote the system of sacrifices by the people, he spoke out, "According to scripture, my house will be a house of prayer. But you have turned it into a robbers' den."

In the few days that followed, Jesus came to the temple each day. The temple officials, who did not dare to seize him in front of the crowds, tried to trap him with questions. But he stood up to them, giving answers that amazed and delighted the crowds. He went right on teaching the people, retiring each night with his disciples to their hiding place in the Garden of Gethsemane. Then, two days before Passover, Jesus planned the traditional supper in Jerusalem with his disciples. In the same clairvoyant way he had used before, he chose the room where they met. They ate the unleavened bread and shared a cup of wine in sorrow, because Jesus told the twelve that this would be their last meal together. He compared it to his own body and blood, and said that one of them was about to betray him.

Then as night fell, Judas stole away to tell the temple guard where Jesus could be found that night, and received his thirty pieces of silver. The rest of the group sang as they went to the Garden of Gethsemane where Jesus wanted to pray. He asked three of them to watch with him. But instead they went to sleep. Alone he met the full onslaught of evil, sweating blood as he asked that this cup might be taken from him, yet making no move to escape. When Judas and the temple guard were near, Jesus awakened the disciples. They saw him seized, and then one by one they fled. Only Peter followed his master at a distance, and by morning, as Jesus had predicted, Peter had three times denied even knowing him.

Before the High Priest and the Sanhedrin Jesus was accused by contradictory witnesses and charged. He claimed to be equal with God, they charged, and under Jewish law he deserved to die. He was taunted and struck, and at daybreak he was handed over to the governor for execution. Before Pilate Jesus stood with courage and dignity. Pilate wanted to release him, as was his right at the Passover if the people wished it. But the crowd, egged on by the High Priest and elders, demanded Barrabas, and Jesus was condemned to die on the cross.

He was first flogged by the soldiers and then forced to carry the beam of his cross to the place of crucifixion. There he was crucified between two thieves. He spoke only a few times and then died. Since the religious leaders did not want the Passover sabbath defiled by bodies hanging there, an order was given to kill the prisoners. There was surprise that Jesus was already dead, and a lance was thrust into his side. Joseph of Arimathaea obtained permission to take the body. He removed it quickly to his own tomb. Before the sun set and the sabbath began, while some of the women watched, Jesus' body was placed in the tomb.

Men and women have meditated over this life for

nearly two millennia. Even the most critical agree that here was one of the best of men, courageous, concerned, loving, powerful in word and action. It is difficult to pick flaws in the character of this man. He was strong and courageous, yet understanding and loving, the perfect balance of what a man ought to be. And yet the best of men met the worst of deaths. His life ended in condemnation, mockery and torture. If this was the end, what was its purpose? And yet this is where the popular presentations of the Christian message leave the story, presentations like *Godspell* and *Jesus Christ Superstar*.

Resurrection

But the most startling thing about the story is that this was not the end. Apparently Jesus rose from the dead. He appeared to Peter and the rest of the remaining eleven. He appeared to Mary Magdalene and some of the other women. Then he appeared to more than five hundred of his followers, many of whom Paul said were still living when he wrote his letter to the Corinthians twenty years later. After that he did not appear in the same dramatically physical sense, but his presence continued to be intensely real. He was alive for Christians in the early church, and through the Holy Spirit gave them the power to continue on the way he had opened up for them.

In scarcely three hundred years the disciples, the little band of unknown men in an out-of-the-way land, had left their mark on every corner of the great Roman Empire. The number of followers had grown until they were spread out all over the ancient world. In spite of almost constant persecution as an illegal and forbidden religion, Christianity was about to become the official religion of the Empire. As one writer has remarked, these men and women of the early church outlived, outfought, and out-died the ancient world. And they testified to the reality, the new power which supported them in every way. As followers of Jesus of Nazareth, who could share in his resurrected life, they were able to continue the same ministry of teaching, preaching about the kingdom, and healing. They were often known as "the followers of the Way."

Thus the early church believed that Jesus continued to teach them through the Holy Spirit, and they often found these direct teachings just as true and important as those which Jesus had given as historical man. This creates a problem which has been opened up by historical criticism of the gospels. It asks: How can we know which facts in the gospels belong to the actual history of the man Jesus, and which ones came from the action of the Spirit working in the church? Much of this historical and textual criticism has been excellent and was needed. But when thinkers began to reject the recorded facts wholesale, the reasons they developed had very little to do with good historical methods. Many of them would be humorous if the results were not so tragic.[2]

The facts of Jesus' life are a matter of *history,* set down in records that were written to tell, as best they knew how, what had happened. They also repeat the myth of the dying and rising God. There is no good reason why history should not investigate these facts, including the events of that first Easter, and the actual resurrection of Jesus of Nazareth and his appearance to his disciples. These events either happened, or they did not, and there is no particular historical reason to reject them. As we have seen, the best recent studies show that there is a basis of solid fact in the gospel, and that we should think twice before rejecting parts of it offhand.

Still, it is quite possible for a person to believe in the historical fact of Easter without finding it meaningful in his own life. It can be accepted as history and still be no

more significant than, say, the murder of Julius Caesar.
If Easter is accepted in this way—as an event that happened once upon a time, but too far from us to have much
present-day significance or meaning—then one pays lip
service to Christianity and has a conventional, intellectual
faith. This is the way most modern Christian churches
accept Easter, if they accept it at all. Yet does this kind
of Christianity have real significance? What is the meaning of these events unless they were the first breakthrough
of the Spirit which is still trying to come into our lives
and transform them?

To the early Christians Jesus not only proclaimed
the kingdom of God, he lived it. His life was the prime
example of its presence and power. And in his resurrection the kingdom had broken fully into history. The cross
and the death of Jesus, they saw, were the worst that the
Evil One could do to interfere with the kingdom of God.
But in the resurrection Christ triumphed over the powers
of evil and death, and the kingdom had a beachhead on
a new country—a country which, until then, had been
largely dominated by the powers of the Evil One. Now
it was a matter of following up the victory which had
been won.

One might say that in the early church Christianity
equaled Easter. This, in fact, was the point Paul made to
the Corinthians; after taking up their specific problems
and the need to deal with them, this was his clinching
argument. For these Christians Easter was the verification
of the power of God's kingdom over Satan's domain. Men
no longer had to fear evil. Its power had been broken.
Even when it struck men then and there, in one of the
provinces of the Roman Empire, they knew they were
freed from its power in the life after death. The value of
Christianity, the very reasons for believing it, were linked
irretrievably with the truth of the resurrection and Easter.

In reality, Easter can have significance only in this

kind of spiritual context, a mythological context. Its importance to men lies in the defeat of powers which have a decided influence over their lives. Easter has meaning because it opens up the reality of a different kind of spiritual power, that of God, breaking into the physical world in a victory over evil and death. Otherwise, if Easter is simply the story of a resuscitated corpse, it is not very edifying. If one does not believe or know the reality of these powers, if he cannot see the resurrection as their breakthrough into space and time, then he will certainly not find much significance in that event. He is more likely to negate any new power that does try to touch him and keep it from being effective.

The trouble is that when men believe only in a material world and in the power of reason to keep it explainable and in working order, they have no context in which to accept the unique meaning of Christianity and Easter. Nor do they have any place for the healings and visions, the angelic powers and miracles which abound in the life of Jesus. No wonder they turn away from Christianity. It is the sensible thing to do if one is sure there is nothing but a material world. As for the message of Easter, what place could it have?

Men who believe in this way may accept the truth of what once happened, but so what? Jesus of Nazareth, a good man, infused with the spirit of God in a unique way, died. And through some action of God he was raised from the dead. He was resuscitated. Christ showed Pilate that he had a power which even the Roman Empire could not defeat, and his rising mocked the chief priests who had brought him to death. From these facts certain other ideas can be inferred, but there the power of the event ceases. We may really believe that God demonstrated what he could do in the resurrection and so he must actually be in heaven, even though we are not able to feel it ourselves most of the time or to have any feeling that he will ever share with us the benefits of that power. We may even have the intellectual certainty that God can work, though he doesn't do it very often now; and this kind of thinking may give a certain intellectual confidence. But even among the most logical and consistent people (and few of us are that logical and consistent), this does not make for a very powerful or vital religious life. That comes from a different kind of belief in Easter.

To the authors of the New Testament and to the church fathers Easter was more than a single historical event, more than simply a demonstration that God could break through space and time and causality. To them Easter was a spiritual victory over metaphysically real evil forces. To be freed from domination by these forces men had only to claim the victory which had been won for them. Gustav Aulén, in his little book *Christus Victor,* has shown how real this faith was for the first six centuries of the church's life. Redemption or salvation was not a logical idea, but an experiential fact. And these men knew what they needed to be saved from. It was called death, in the sense of destructive negativity. Both in the New Testament and to the church fathers the word *death* meant an uncreative force which exists in the world, a destroying aspect of reality which often possesses and uses men as its tool.

It was this *death* that Jesus defeated on that first Easter. He called a halt to the inevitable ravages of evil, to the effectiveness of the Evil One in this world. This victory could be appropriated by men if they would follow him and be filled with his spirit. This, it was believed, was a metaphysical and mythological fact which could only be described in image and story. It was this which Paul described in the fifteenth chapter of I Corinthians: " 'Death is swallowed up; victory is won!' 'O Death, where is your victory? O Death, where is your sting?' The sting of death is sin, and sin gains its power from the law; but,

God be praised, he gives us the victory through our Lord
Jesus Christ."

If Easter and Christianity are to be truly meaningful,
crucially meaningful for us today, then we must be able
to see this event within a spiritual and mythological framework in which man can still find meaning today. And this
takes some doing, since most of our culture today, both
secular and religious, is engulfed by the same materialistic
mythology in which both positivism and Marxism are
rooted. In order to discover the full significance of Easter,
it is necessary to see through the current mythology of
materialism and consider three propositions.

We need to be able, first, to consider the possibility
that, alongside the material world, there is a world of
spiritual reality that is both positive and negative—from
a human point of view, both good and evil—and that both
aspects have a profound effect upon men's lives and on
their world. Next, we need to entertain the hypothesis that
these powers can break through into history and manifest
themselves in a most concrete way, again for good *or* evil.
And third we need to be willing to try out in action the
proposition that Jesus, the Christ, met and defeated these
spiritual powers of evil in his death and resurrection, and
that he makes his victory available to those who understand how to follow him.

We have seen the mythological powers of death and
destruction break through the minds of imbalanced men,
leaving their imprint on the history of our own nation.
We who are Christian in reality as well as in name are
given the way to deal with these powers, the very forces
which destroyed both Lincoln and Kennedy. Christ fell
victim to them, and then rose victorious over them. The
man who follows Christ, and who is willing consciously
to face and acknowledge these same forces within the
depths of himself, is then able to confront them. Through
Christ's victory, he is given the power to identify and then

deal with these powers of destruction, without being swamped by them.

The New Testament story tells of this spiritual victory and then how it was lived out by those people in the first century. The victory was realized concretely in the lives of very real people. Its transforming power remains conclusive in the realm of spirit, and is just as available to us as it ever was, once we learn how to seek it. This victory—which seems to have failed both Lincoln and Kennedy, as well as so many others, when they needed it most—is ours to seek and unlock. Nothing then need defeat us. Nothing in death or life, in the realm of spirits or superhuman powers, in the world as it is or the world as it shall be, in the forces of the universe, in heights or depths—nothing in all creation, as Paul put it, need defeat us if we find this relation to God through Christ.

Let us now turn to see what sense we can make of the spiritual world and the mythology which expresses it. Is there any evidence in our world for the reality of spirit or any real way of understanding its expression in myths and images?

VI

Some Misconceptions about Myth

Before we go on to show how myth can be used by the modern Christian, we need to clear up some misconceptions and misunderstandings. These one-sided ideas about myth are all around us today. We hope to show in the following pages that myth has a practical use today and that mythical thinking is a helpful and legitimate activity which often leads to genuine knowledge.

In recent years there has been no lack of interest in myth. This subject, that was once the exclusive domain of Bulfinch and the poets, is receiving serious study in one area after another of our modern culture. Today there are studies of myth being done by sociologists and philologists, by social psychologists, students of folklore, and now and then even philosophers. Literary critics and students of art, education, comparative religion, and culture examine the part myth has played in the building of civilization. Archaeologists and ethnographers are adding their discoveries, while historians and even journalists take pages to detail the myth-making process in the life of some individual or other.

Each of the groups has contributed important insights to this study. Yet no one of them is primarily concerned with man's use of myth and its practical value for his life. Each of these branches of learning necessarily works within its own field of interest, using its own expert knowledge and tools of investigation. And (except for certain men in psychology, which is considered a similarly limited field of knowledge), no one group in our society has a special stake in understanding what is being learned about myth, and seeing how it can be used in man's life today. It is quietly assumed that myth can have no practical value for the present day.[1]

A great deal of valuable information is amassed, particularly about the relation of myth to primitive arts and earlier cultures. But there the effort ends, and another idea or bit of information is tucked away into its proper academic cubbyhole—perhaps along with "ancient Mayan techniques of farming," or "early Etruscan figurines," or even "the effect of Freud on Broadway"—and there it is left to ferment on its own. Hardly anyone stops to ask if our understanding of myth affects anything but the arts and techniques which seem to be so important to man. Whose business is it then to help man himself approach and deal with myth?

Myth and the Practical Profession of Religion

The suggestion I have to make is that one of the principal purposes of religion is to help men approach and work with myth. As strange as this will sound to modern ears, what I am saying is that myth and religion are both very practical matters for man's life. The biased attitude of our modern materialistic world against both myth and religion has affected us all, whether we realize it or not. And the effort to recapture man's natural approach to religion, his natural feeling and need for it, goes hand in hand with a grasp of the reality of myth. If myth makes a real difference in human life how can we understand its practical function?

Probably the first thing to realize is that myth and ritual are actually two side-by-side avenues leading to the same reality. Myth describes in words a pattern of images which has important meaning, and ritual is the way of expressing such a pattern by acting it out. Through ritual and ceremony, in rite and liturgy, one steps directly into the mythological pattern and expresses its meaning with sacred play. Myth which is not acted out in some way is almost incomplete. Myth is the idea or symbol of the reality and its meaning; ritual action is its embodiment. By the same token, all real play—any action that is truly playful—expresses some of the same quality of worship and ritual.[2] In the pages that follow, when we speak of myth, we will be referring not only to the spoken or written pattern of images, but to the lived myth of ritual and ceremony as well.

It is not hard to see the importance of myth if we believe that man is surrounded by nonphysical realities which play upon his life fully as much as the physical world around him, and that through myth and ritual he is given contact with these realities. Almost all people around the world until recent times have believed that these nonphysical or spiritual powers constitute the more important half of man's total environment. The way they affect him often determines how he approaches the physical world and whether he is lackadaisical or enthusiastic in his relationships in it. Through myth and ritual man is offered understanding of the spiritual powers around him and this in itself helps a great deal in relating to them.

What is more important, the contact with these nonphysical realities opens new avenues of knowledge to man, as well as giving him fresh insights about the world and new ways of dealing with it. It also releases hidden springs of energy in him, and the religious approach through myth and ritual offers him needed protection from the malignant forces found along with the helpful powers. One of the primary functions of the religious profession—the profession of priest, of shaman or seer or religious leader by whatever name he is called—is to provide an experience of this kind of relationship with spiritual reality. This has been the understanding of practically every religion of which we have any real knowledge, including Christianity during most of its history.

But when I came to realize the importance of myth and ritual in my own religious profession, oddly enough it was not through the Christian church. My own realization of the importance of myth and a religious approach to it came through the studies of psychologists who were followers of Carl Jung. Through their efforts to restore emotionally sick people to health, to help people over their anxieties, hang-ups and mental quirks, these men found that religion is not just a nicety to add to an already mature life. The truly religious approach to life is not just a perfume which one adds to a well-bathed life, but the bath itself. It is the way man finds his bearings, his direction and meaning in life.

What these psychologists found is that the sense of loss of meaning could result in a host of psychological and physical illnesses. Although not all psychological illness has this root, the loss of direction and purpose is often a common cause of such illness in the modern world. And they discovered that one way men could be brought to a sense of meaning, and thus to health, was to bring them into an experience of the positive side of spiritual reality—an experience of the central reality of which all the major religions of mankind speak. This reconnecting was only possible as men began to discover how to use myth and ritual once again. In this way, by being escorted over the narrow boundary between psychology, philosophy and religion, a great many people have become aware of the importance of myth, and so discovered the value of a religious approach to it. In many cases these have been people who were as critical in their thinking as any others in our society. We shall have more to say later about the psychological understanding of myth and what the thinking of Dr. Jung offers to Christians.

What I have to say, however, is as a representative of religion, and more specifically as a representative of one particular religious heritage, Christianity. As I wrote these words I realized that my materialistic brainwashing makes me feel defensive when I have no reason to feel that way about being a Christian. One has only to stop and realize the inner meaning and power that our religion offers. By realizing the mythological understanding it offers, we can see how realistically Christianity approaches the world without omitting or denying any area of men's experience of it. I certainly don't know of any other religious heritage that offers men as complete an understanding of their world, or a better method of dealing with it. On the other hand, I doubt if Christianity can be effective in the modern world until it discovers again the place of myth in man's understanding of the universe and learns to appreciate the use of myth. My interest in this subject is in enabling us Christians, myself included, to find more of the vitality and sustaining power which was known in the first vital centuries of the church's life.

Religion is essentially a practical matter, strange as this may sound to men brought up in today's materialistic world with its prejudices against anything that seems to lack "substance." There are even men today like Dietrich Bonhoeffer who find so little practical value in religion that they say man needs a "religionless religion." Yet the purpose of religion is to help men deal with life. Thus religion views mythology from the point of view of what it can do, rather than as a subject in itself. Religion is interested in the practical use of myth.

In fact, the religious study of myth might be compared with engineering. Like the engineer who puts the studies and researches of the pure sciences to use, the worshiping group and the priest make use of the elements of myth which are discussed by other specialists in order to produce an effect on man's environment. Myth gives man some handle on a vast, almost unknown environment of nonphysical reality that surrounds him. Where the engineer is seeking a direct result in the physical world, the religious group looks for a positive relationship with a nonphysical realm of being which has a significant influence on people's lives. Both are looking for results, and in the long run these results usually overlap in each realm. Sooner or later, religion which is effective will have practical results in the material world. To suggest how this happens in a concrete way let us consider two examples in which lives were altered by a personal understanding of ancient and non-Christian mythological motifs, and then two in which specifically Christian symbolism made the difference.

One of them was a man who came to me because of almost intolerable fears which blocked his attempts to meet other people on their own ground. His life had been a series of personal skirmishes with parents and friends, from which he always seemed to come off second best, pressured and clinging to whatever authority was at hand. As a result he was cut off from his own potential. He lacked, as he put it, either the accomplishment or the sense of personal satisfaction which others appeared to find in life. But for a number of years he had been expressing his feelings through painting. Working entirely on his own, he had produced several pictures that represented ancient mythological themes. He did not know why he had painted them, but eventually, bit by bit, he came to see that they had significance in relation to his own life. By understanding their meaning, he was able to come to terms with his fears, thus resolving many of his basic problems so that he could find deeper relationships with other people.

About the same time a young man came to me who was actually paralyzed by his fears. He was unable to move in any direction. Because he had been—as mythology would express it—"swallowed by the mother," his own creative abilities were trapped and could not be lived out. One day we happened to talk about the Venus-Adonis myth, and suddenly he caught its meaning. First, he went home and started a large painting of the dying Adonis. Simply by working on it, he felt something of the same freedom from the mother complex, something almost like a death within himself. Then he did an abstract sculpture of the same theme. In this way he was able to express what he experienced and to become at least partially free. These two creative expressions, together with an understanding of the material, released him to step into a more masculine role and to become a healthier and more independent person. This myth, and the ritual of expressing it, changed his life.

For another person a simple Christian ritual was enough to start a change. This was a woman in middle life who was struggling with deep depressions. At times it seemed that dark forms might engulf and destroy her. The psychiatrist she was seeing, with whom I was in close contact, was very worried about the possibility of a psychotic break. He encouraged her to see me. As we talked, I found that she had been trying to face her darkness directly and deal singlehandedly with the destructive powers of the psyche. But facing these depths was something she could not do at that time. Instead, her task was to build a bulwark against these dark and threatening forces and not be overwhelmed by them. I suggested that she wear a small cross around her neck and, instead of exposing herself to these forces when she was invaded by them, that she fight them off by taking hold of the cross and remembering how the forces of darkness were defeated there. With this simple use of the Christian myth, she found stability and continued to grow and develop without a psychotic break.

A second application of the Christian myth was more complex. This was a man in his middle thirties, with deep Christian roots, who was subject to severe anxiety attacks and recurrent depression. He was also working with a psychiatrist and, without being specific, we both encouraged him to see what these agitated moods looked like in images. He began to set down in writing the images that came to him. It appeared as if a powerful witch came and stood over him, sometimes screaming that he had no value, or sometimes attacking him in vividly physical ways.

As he continued to work with these images, we talked now and then about Christian rituals of redemption. One day he saw the witch-figure poised to attack him, and suddenly felt that he was holding a bucket of water in his hand. He saw that he could give one mighty effort and heave the water, bucket and all, at the figure. As he did, he heard within him the words, "I baptize you in the name of the Father . . ." With that, the figure slowly dissolved before his eyes, and from that point on his anxiety began to lift. He was able to confront an attack imaginatively, usually calling the Christ to enter the scene himself and offer rescue and also his caring concern. In this way, this one individual found the immediate meaning for him of the Christian story of redemption from such destructive forces of evil. He was soon free of depression and anxiety and able to go on with his busy and creative life with real zest once again.

These are four examples of people living in the present day who came to understand the meaning of myth and applied this understanding to their own lives. As they did so, they found most of their problems reduced to manageable size so that they were freed to live more creatively. Need I say that they took religion quite seriously after that. And this is only a sampling from one individual's personal experience.

Wherever this practice has been known, the same kind of results are found. It makes little difference whether one calls it religion or psychology. The effect on people's lives is the same whether the experiences are recorded in the history of the Christian church, or in the twenty volumes of C. G. Jung's *Collected Works* and the dozens of others by his followers. The same transformation and healing have taken place in all the great religious revivals from the early church to Methodism and Pentecostalism. These results have occurred, and they still occur, when religion and its mythology become alive and real for people. Few books have described this better than William James' classic work, *The Varieties of Religious Experience.*

It would be a good idea, then, for us to try to understand these stories which are called myth. Just what is the meaning of myth and ritual which gives them this power to touch and change lives? How do they fit into our over-all understanding of human life? First of all, we need to see how our ordinary ways of thinking differ from the imagination involved in myth, and how these two approaches to reality are related.

Two Kinds of Thinking

Man has two ways of expressing meaning. He can do it by using the thoughts and ideas and concepts which he has developed, or he can use symbols and images to convey meaning. Most of us have been so thoroughly trained to try to use logical concepts and the analytical method of thinking that we almost forget that there is another valid way to express meaning. And it is a very different process from the method of logical thought or reason.

We must never belittle the value of this method, however. Logical thinking has given us the great bulk of our science and technology, our medicine and formal arts. Without it we would have no higher mathematics or computer science, and little of the social sciences, or metaphysics and rational theology. It has enriched our lives in countless ways. Many of us would not even be alive to read these pages without miracle drugs, anesthesia and modern surgery. But as we rejoice in the benefits of the analytical method, we must remember that it has also provided the atom bomb and chemical warfare, at the same time doing little to deter the Western nations from their nearly suicidal struggles of the last seventy years. Although logical thought is valuable and important, fortunately it does not exhaust our capacity to convey meaning—nor does it touch the deepest recesses of men's hearts.

Thinking which is effective in this way is found when man also uses his ability to think through images and symbols, through stories and myths. And this way is basically different from logical reasoning, which is usually forced and takes concentrated, conscious effort. Instead there is an effortless flow to thinking in pictures and images. It can almost be said to go on within us, rather than our causing it. Man can develop and nurture this kind of thinking, and to a certain extent he can direct it, but he does not create it. Man develops meaning in this way much as a miner finds valuable ore, or a farmer brings crops from the soil. Once the meaning has been brought out or harvested, he can go on developing it through logical thinking, like an artisan shaping a tool, or a mechanic building a machine. But to replenish the supply, he must go back to this basic way in which meaning is first expressed.

Logical thinking was a relatively late comer to the stage of civilized life. It was developed first among the Greeks in the fifth and fourth centuries B.C. Yet man has always known how to convey meaning through images. One of the real fictions we have been taught is that when the Greeks developed rational thought they turned their backs upon mythological thinking. Nothing could be farther from the truth. Except for Aristotle, who tried to do just that, the leaders of Greek thought all combined rational and mythological thinking and found no contradiction.[3] The foundations of modern thought were laid during centuries when Christians went on developing this understanding. Almost until modern times it was fully realized that man needs both symbolic thinking and rational thinking. But then the Western world, as we shall see, came under the sway of Aristotle and the idea grew that man had to make a choice between myth and logic.

Yet thinking in images or mythological thinking seems to spring out of the very nature of man himself. There are no records of man so archaic that they do not show man conveying meaning through images, nor any culture so modern that it does not know the mysterious ability of images to stir up meaning and emotion in the hearer. For as long as we know men have been telling stories to express meaning. And, barring some disaster to our ability to communicate, they will continue to tell stories or myths which convey meaning, not logically but through the power of symbol and imagination. Looked at logically, however, these stories do not reveal their meaning. Man listens, but he does not hear, because the significance of myth cannot be grasped when men are unable to look beyond the narrative facts of a story and their logical meaning. It is not a question of either/or. Man needs both kinds of thinking to deal with the total world.

Different Kinds of Stories

Many people are afraid of myth because they confuse

it with superstition, which tends to see every mythical idea as an actual historical event. This is clearly absurd. But when the religious group has no understanding of myth as referring to the nonphysical or spiritual world, then one is faced with the alternative of either considering all myth as religious nonsense, or of regarding it superstitiously as telling of outer, physical events. If one is to avoid superstition and grant myth a realistic place in religion, then it is necessary to realize that some events are primarily historical, some are primarily mythical (in the sense of nonphysical happenings), and some are historical enactments of mythical patterns, which occur when the two realms cross and merge.

Besides this, there are many different kinds of stories. Some, of course, are simple historical accounts; one listens to a factual recital of events, or studies it for an exam and then promptly forgets the names or places or dates. These stories scarcely touch one at all. Sometimes the material of a story is selected simply to amuse or divert, like a good who-done-it, with little or no significance in the material itself. Then there are stories that are told for some ego purpose, put together to convince the hearer of some point of view; this is the essence of the sales pitch, which may be pure fiction or fabrication based on some fact. Studies of communication show that it is easier to reach a man through images and stories than by logical argument. A story will be remembered, while the logical ideas flow in one ear and out the other. Modern advertising techniques have developed this use of images to a fine point.

Many stories are told for the direct emotional effect they have on both the teller and the reader, and there is good reason for this. Images have the same capacity to stimulate emotion as actual events. And it is well known that emotion is an agent of change in human beings. Emotion helps to arouse the individual to action, and undoubtedly this is a large element of man's myths. Studies show that there is a close relation between intense emotion and religious experience. Perhaps this explains why a society which is dubious about myth also distrusts human emotion.[4] This is beginning to change, however, starting in the schools where educators find that learning is greatly increased when imagery with emotional value is used to reinforce the educational process.[5]

Finally there are the stories which are our interest, the ones that are called saga or legend or myth. These stories arouse emotion but they also strike something even deeper within the hearer. They move both the teller and the hearer, striking at the very meaning, the roots of life. While the quality of such a story is difficult to explain in ordinary words, it is often expressed by being acted out. Myths, in fact, often make such a profound impression that they almost require some kind of acted response, a dance, a ritual, some action to express the emotions which have been generated and released.

This kind of story may appear to be the imaginative production of the storyteller, but looking more deeply one realizes that the story seems to be telling itself through him, while he is only the agent through which it is expressed. Many psychologists believe that imaginative writing reveals depths within the individual far beyond the conscious intent and personal psychology of the writer. *Dr. Jekyll and Mr. Hyde,* for instance, may tell us things about Robert Louis Stevenson, or *Wuthering Heights* about Emily Brontë, that the writers were only dimly aware of themselves. Like poets, they wrote because there was something demanding to be expressed; in the case of *Dr. Jekyll and Mr. Hyde,* in fact, the demand was made in a dream so strongly that Stevenson could not rest until it was written out.

Sometimes the teller may be recalling some story from history which has a similar effect upon the hearer, which makes a similar demand and requires the same response.

What makes a story mythical is not its source—whether it is conce'ved in imagination or springs out of history—but its significance and meaning, its impact, its effectiveness in touching your life and mine. It may seem that we are belaboring the point, but this is one of the most essential points we have to make. A myth may be either an imaginative production or an account of actual historical happenings. The test is whether it stirs the depth of man and calls up emotion and response in a way that shows that it comes from beyond the ordinary physical world, from a reality of spirit.

So often myth is considered simply an interesting story which is not true and yet this idea misses the truth entirely. The mythological is not the untrue or unhistorical but rather that which is constantly working in man's life, that which can and sometimes does become historical truth. Myths stir up and reveal meanings, either within the individual or the group, which show another level of reality impinging upon man and affecting his life in many ways. Thus the distinction between fact and fancy, between the historically true and the fabricated, is not the fundamental mark of mythology. The essential characteristic of myth is that it fires the deepest levels of man's psyche and sets off a chain reaction which can and sometimes does work in history by transforming lives emotionally and spiritually.

All great literature shares in this mythological reality. Cervantes, Tolstoy, Chaucer, Bunyan draw upon it. In T. S. Eliot's *Murder in the Cathedral* one finds myth and history all rolled into one. Shakespeare's plays, both tragedies and comedies, have this mythological quality whether they are intended as history or full-fledged imagination. As for the specifically Christian myth, one of the best expressions that has ever been produced is found in Dante's *Divine Comedy*. And for today, the reality of the incarnation is best revealed, not by theology, but by C. S. Lewis' story for children, *The Lion, the Witch and the Wardrobe*. The hunger of today's college students for the reality of myth has made Tolkien's saga of the hobbit one of the most popular works of our time, with its expression of the age old myths in a new garb. Over and over one finds this rising interest in myth and mythical stories, and not just for children, as men realize how much this part of them needs to be fed.

Myth and Man's Knowledge

Some people, following an opposite vein, have argued that mythology was merely primitive man's way of explaining the world we live in. According to this point of view these stories grew up before men had developed the capacity to think logically, and so they reassured themselves, for instance, that the sun would rise each morning by repeating the myth of Phoebus Apollo carrying the sun in his winged boat. And to remember the change of seasons they invented stories of a dying and rising god. But as man came of age and was able to use his reason, mythology then became only a curiosity to be put aside like a childish thing or an outmoded garment.

This was the idea of Auguste Comte and particularly of James Frazer who spent a lifetime studying and classifying primitive and ancient myths. Although one wonders why so much effort was spent on something of so little importance, their ideas did not stop there. They were picked up uncritically by Edmund Husserl who passed them on to the modern European philosophical tradition and so, through Bultmann, Bonhoeffer and Tillich, to modern Christian theology. And in just this way a great many serious Christians were led to turn their backs on mythology. The reader who wants the whole sad story can get it in the first six chapters of my recent book *Encounter with God*.

Perhaps primitive man did devise some myths in order to explain the world in which he lived (or more likely to express his wonder at it), but this certainly does not exhaust the meaning of myths. Some of the greatest thinkers of all times have recognized that there comes a time when rational, logical thought comes up against problems which cannot be unraveled by reason alone, and so they turn to myth and mythological thinking to discover the meaning they are trying to open up.

We find Plato in the fourth century B.C. turning to mythological figures to explain the nature of the soul. He describes it as a chariot drawn by two horses, one white and one black, pulling in opposition, with the task of the driver (the center of the personality) to control and balance his steeds. In another place Plato tells the myth of the cave to picture the way we human beings receive intimations of truth from beyond this sensory world. Both Plato and Socrates found it necessary to use myth in order to describe adequately the nature of the world that surrounds man.[6] The great philosopher of modern Spain, Unamuno, after attempting to discuss the origin of human weakness and sin in his book *The Tragic Sense of Life,* turns to the mythological story of the garden of Eden as the best explanation he can give. Only this story does justice to the complexity of the problem.

These men were not abandoning their rational thought processes. Nor can it be considered that they were reverting to a primitive method in these passages, or that such thinking reveals a lack of logic. These men, rather, had stretched rational thought to its limit. Plato and Socrates, in fact, were the very men who developed rational thought as few others have done in any age. But when the thread of logic would stretch no further, they then put myth to work to give form to the further knowledge of reality and experience and meaning so that it could then be discussed and better understood.

There is interesting support for this understanding of myth from perhaps the least expected source—the philosophy of science. With the development of nuclear physics (by the 1930s), men began to know enough about the universe to realize that they had only a partial understanding of it, and that they probably never would understand it fully. Some of these scientists have even suggested that the only understanding they have is derived from the models they make of what they think exists. The more accurate the model, the more adequate is our understanding. And just how is a model so different from a myth? Both are pictures intended to convey some understanding of reality.

The most dramatic suggestion has been made by the philosopher of science, Paul Feyerabend. He maintains that the crucial element in scientific discovery is not clear rational thought, but imagination. Without the capacity to imagine, to think in images, Feyerabend shows, the scientist has no way to perceive the structure of things as they are. Nor can he break out of his old conceptions even when some new fact is staring him in the face. The way Albert Einstein arrived at his discoveries is certainly rather conclusive evidence of this.

It would appear that, for no reason at all, a great many of us have been limiting ourselves to a very narrow band of experience. The thinkers who have insisted that man is limited to logical thought based only on sense experience have thus denied one of the most valuable ways we have of coming to know ourselves and the realities around us. And strangely enough, these thinkers believe they are being "scientific," and yet fail entirely to account for scientific creativity. By denying the validity of symbolic and mythological thinking, they have succeeded in making man less than he really is.

Many myths do contain certain primitive and archaic elements, but the great, persistent mythological motifs also lay open meanings and powers that are beyond the reach of logical thinking. These myths are the very bone and muscle of religion and the religious way. They speak to the religious problems of life when logic fails to give even a basis for discussing many of those problems. Since man is more than logic, and myth expresses that more, men do not become free of superstition by avoiding myth. They then allow their method of investigation to determine the way reality appears to them, rather than looking at all the facts, and this is a very questionable scientific procedure.

From the more complete point of view I am suggesting, myth is seen as one of the ways meaning is provided for a nation or a culture, much as certain other experiences do this for the individual. Since this way of looking at myth has grown out of a religious understanding of the world, it is very different from the view of many nineteenth century thinkers. At that time, when meaning enough was being found in the material world, it was easy to look down on myths as a quaint way of making up for lack of scientific understanding. But as some of the most creative thinkers in the modern world have begun to struggle with man's problems and confusion, they find that myth must be considered very seriously today if people are to understand themselves and their world again.

These men are returning to an understanding of man much like that of Plato and Augustine. And these are careful thinkers who are well aware of their reasons for such an approach. They find that meaning seems to come to man from beyond the physical world, or that it cannot be explained only in terms of physical reality. Therefore, man needs a way of expressing and giving form to these patterns of meaning so that he can grasp and use them. And this is the function of myth, which makes mythology as necessary to twentieth century scientific man as it was in ancient times.

VII

Psychology,
Philosophy and Myth

In a world which had valued practically nothing but logical thinking and the cold facts of sense experience for centuries, it is no wonder that mythology was disowned, and that Western Christianity has allowed its mythological life to die of starvation. Western man, religious or not, came to believe that he was nothing but a shell of mechanically functioning matter, built to house his rational consciousness. The only important part of man was the logical awareness which helped him understand the material world of which he was one small part. This attitude was well expressed by thinkers at the beginning of the twentieth century; it became the assumed, popular base for most Western thinking. We live in a self-contained, material universe, with no cracks that would allow anything else to break through into it. Probably no one else said it better than Karl Marx and B. F. Skinner.[1]

Strangely enough, just as people were trying to get used to that kind of world, science began to see it differently. The explorers in science, men who were making the discoveries, realized that they were not so sure about things; they did not know as much as they had thought. Beginning with Mme. Curie and Einstein, they were finding that the scientific truths they had once considered universal and absolutely certain were only partly true. They were beginning to see more deeply into the secrets of the universe than men had ever dreamed of. But to those in the front ranks, it was not only clear that there were many things science did not know; there were even limits to what men could expect to learn through science. Because of this scientific revolution, which I have described in some detail in my book *Encounter with God,* leaders in one area after another questioned the idea that man finds himself in a world moved only by physical forces. Once man no longer thinks that he knows *all* about his universe, it is only by *faith* that he maintains his materialistic conviction.

As the physicist Werner Heisenberg remarks, science has become skeptical of its own skepticism. In *Science and Philosophy,* Heisenberg, who shaped our understanding of the atom, stresses the importance of ideas like *God* and the *human soul.* He points out that because these words come from the natural language, they describe reality and our experience of it better than any of the exact definitions of mathematics or physics or chemistry. Others, including Robert Oppenheimer, detail the change in physics from a study of only objects that could be measured to an attempt to understand the various forces that move through reality.

The mind of science itself has been changed by success. Stephen Toulmin suggests that scientific laws are only maps to help us get around in reality, not exact statements of what things are. We have already mentioned the work of Paul Feyerabend of the University of California. He goes on to suggest to scientists that they must develop imagination if scientific discovery is to continue. Feyerabend realizes how much science depends upon the kind of imagination that helped Kekulé make the first real breakthrough in organic chemistry. Kekulé had been trying to figure out how the atoms could fit together to form benzene. After working hard on the problem, he was dozing on a bus ride in Southern France when he suddenly saw the image of six snakes, each swallowing the tail of the next to form a circle, and realized that this was his clue to the structure of the benzene ring—a hint of its six carbon atoms linked in the form of a hexagon. This was the beginning of organic chemistry as we know it today.

And one of the world's greatest mathematicians, Kurt Gödel, has shown that even mathematics is not absolutely certain. It is based, according to him, upon man's intuition of mathematical realities and so is essentially perceptive in nature. He even suggests that these mathematical realities may exist apart from anything that could be counted, very much as Plato suggested that "Ideas" exist apart from physical reality.

It is interesting that medical scientists have also realized the importance of such nonphysical experiences, and are spending time and effort to investigate dreams and other extrasensory perceptions. In addition medicine no longer finds that disease results solely from physical causes, but that man's emotions (which cannot be considered as material) play a part in most of his sickness. Studies of resistance to disease, both bacterial and cancerous, show how much emotion affects the army of white blood cells or lymphocytes. In fact, even faith is now seen as a specific remedy for some illnesses; as one leading professor of psychiatry suggests, there are many cases in which the essence of the patient's illness is fear, and the "mobilization of expectant trust by whatever means may be as much an etiological remedy as penicillin is for pneumonia."[2] Science has even begun to ask how faith comes into being.

Many students of evolution today seriously question whether Darwin's simple theory of evolutional development through survival of the fittest accounts for man's origins. Both Loren Eiseley and the great Jesuit anthropologist Teilhard de Chardin have amassed data which suggests that a purpose is at work in evolution in addition to the blind force of survival. They both see some kind of meaning and direction operating in our world and within us men to make us what we are and what we might become. Studies in biology also show that life does not progress in a steady even flow, but that mutations cause it to progress in jumps and starts.

It is modern depth psychology, however, which has revealed most clearly that man is subject to forces other than material ones, forces and patterns which have a relation to myth. Medical men, who were trying to make sick people well, discovered again that man has layers of personality of which he does not have conscious control, and if a man does not deal with these parts of himself, then he may well become sick. Freud was the first great pioneer in this field. In his *Interpretation of Dreams,* published in 1901, he showed that there are unconscious desires, hopes, longings, ideas and impulses in every man. Even though these are anything but material they are very real. They have an effect upon human lives which can hardly be calculated. It was his discovery and belief that these unconscious realities control more of our behavior than we realize. Our errors, our slips of the tongue and misspoken words, our missed appointments, as well as our neuroses, reveal the presence of the unconscious within us. This unconscious holds attitudes often quite different from that of our conscious minds.

One of the most important ways of understanding the unconscious—indeed, as Freud saw, the royal road to discovering the nature of its contents—is the dream. And what is the dream but a series of images which tell a story? Not every dream, of course; for some are remembered only as fragments which give little more than a rehash of the day before. But there are also dreams which come to nearly every man which tell long and elaborate stories that repeat the great mythological motifs, and this is the characteristic language of dreams. The unconscious reveals its meaning imaginatively, through symbols and images, and it speaks what we have described as a basically mythological language.

Few books have made a greater impact upon our age than Freud's important and basic volume on dreams. If we accept Freud's facts (and there can be little question that those who will read what he says and will look into themselves will find corroboration of them) we will find that there is an element, a deep and necessary part of the human psyche which speaks nearly always in a mythological way. And this part of the psyche, with its profound influence on the whole person, can be reached in stories and images rather than in logical concepts. Freud himself realized the close connection between the dream and mythology, and he called what he considered one of the most important unconscious drives after one of the great Greek myths. He saw in the tragic story of King Oedipus the problem of every human soul which loves the mother because of its nurture in her bosom and must tear himself away from her if it would grow up and mature. The Oedipus complex is the mythological configuration lying at the root of most neuroses, one which expresses itself in many dreams.

According to Freud's understanding, however, the unconscious contained only three basic elements: those things which had been in the individual's consciousness and which had dropped into the unconscious; second, those primal and erotic urges of the *id* which reveal themselves in dreams that seem so strange to the waking mind because they come from this primeval psychic substance; finally, the destructive instincts which pull the individual back into death, into inorganicity, which he called the "death wish." These fragmentary elements from the unconscious seemed to point only to the past and the primitive. But Freud's basic explorations were to be taken a step further by one of his friends and colleagues. This was the Zurich psychiatrist, C. G. Jung.

Jung and Myth

As Jung worked with patients from all over the world, he began to study the mythology of different peoples, even to the extent of personal trips to India, to Africa and to the Indian country in New Mexico and Arizona. He became more and more convinced that the personal dream, the vision, the individual phantasy, and the poetic imagination all revealed a realm of psychic and nonphysical reality which was also spoken of and dealt with in the myths of mankind. Folklore and mythology seemed to have the same significance to the social group that the dream and its associated phenomena had for the individual. Folklore and mythology, then, appeared as the collective dreams of a people, expressing for the group what poetic imagination, phantasies, visions and dreams express for the individual. Both the individual and collective types of experience are vital to human life.

According to Jung dreams have many functions for the individual. They first of all compensate for the one-sided conscious attitude of the individual; in other words these experiences tend to balance a person's conscious, outer life. They also reveal those things of which the individual wishes to remain unaware, confronting him with desires he has not faced up to. But dreams do more than this: they give intimations of meaning and reality which the individual has not as yet touched, and they can even give directions for achieving this meaning and reality.

The dream, in short, reveals one's errors, points to the way of completeness and wholeness and balance, directs how this way can be found, and may even bring one into contact with this reality itself. And according to Jung, the myth does exactly the same thing for the social group. By reflecting the dark, ignored side of the social group, myth reveals the dangers of the group attitudes. It suggests a way to a more complete adaptation to life and reality for the group and it even pictures a method for coming to that wholeness. It also gives contact with the reality of the realm of spirit, particularly in the ritual in which the group shares.

The method suggested by myth for becoming whole or more effective is usually incorporated into the religious ritual of the group, for ritual, as I have already indicated, is actually mythology acted out. Ritual is the response of the group to the myth and through it the myth becomes a living part of each member of the group who participates in it. Undoubtedly this is one reason why, among the many sincere students of mythology, so few are really affected or changed by their study. The myth which becomes a living experience must be participated in. It must be shared in as it was in the Greek drama, in the Hopi snake dance, in the Navajo sand painting, or as in the ancient rites of Attis or the present-day communion service.

The effect of ritual actions does not depend on any understandable or logical reason; these actions are more than logical. Yet they are not *anti*-logical, or *anti*-rational, but *non*rational. They speak to the unconscious depths of the individual, and not just to his conscious mind. Those who try to understand myth or ritual merely by using their rational consciousness will never grasp its significance or meaning. Myth and religious ritual speak to the *un*conscious depths of the individual. They convey meanings which ordinary logical thought cannot convey. They keep the individual and the group in touch with the depths and meanings without which the individual can become sick and the group can disintegrate.

The first book of Dr. Jung's to reach the general public was a volume which appeared in English as *The Psychology of the Unconscious.* Although it is the book he referred to as one of the follies of his youth—written under pressure and too quickly—it was later completely re-edited and published under the title of *Symbols of Transformation*. It is still a difficult book, but it tells a fascinating story. In it Dr. Jung took the visionary experiences of a young woman on the verge of mental illness and traced the mythological content of these images. He showed that these images, which came spontaneously to a mind on the edge of dissolution,* contain most of the important mythological motifs common to mankind. His encyclopedic knowledge of mythology was matched only by his psychological insight and understanding.

Jung's basic conclusion was that the collective unconscious—that depth of the psychic reality which contains more than a personal residue, and which religious people call the realm of spirit—breaks forth in images, symbols, visions, dreams, and myths in order to express its fundamental correction and also its meaning and direction for man. Essentially these are different aspects of the same process of the collective unconscious as it expresses itself through and for men. Later Jung supported this conclusion in his scholarly contributions to the *Essays on a Science of Mythology.*[3]

It was also Jung's finding that men who try to live without contact with the unconscious and its symbolic and mythological meaning often fall sick both psychologically and physically. A great number of his patients came to him suffering from neuroses in which they had lost their sense of meaning in life. Until Jung could help them find contact with their unconscious roots, from which the rational materialism of today had cut them off, they could not get well. In one of his most quoted passages Jung said:

Many hundreds of patients have passed through

---

*These images usually do not get across the threshold of consciousness in sound, healthy minds. Unless a person actively seeks such experiences, his normal thoughts are usually quick to take over and shut out any spontaneous images.

my hands, the greater number being Protestants, a lesser number of Jews, and not more than five or six believing Catholics. Among all my patients in the second half of life—that is to say, over thirty-five—there has not been one whose problem in the last resort was not that of finding a religious outlook on life. It is safe to say that every one of them fell ill because he had lost what the living religions of every age have given to their followers, and none of them has been really healed who did not regain his religious outlook.[4]

Jung was not talking here about intellectual or rational religion, but about religion which deals with images, symbols, rituals, myths. In other words, man cannot remain well psychologically, let alone socially, if he loses contact with the unconscious and its symbolic and mythological life. And the real business of religion, as Jung maintained, is to keep men in touch with this level of reality, and this is done largely through the use of myths.

One interesting confirmation of this viewpoint comes from the widespread dream research being done in laboratories all over the country. The work of William Dement, first at the University of Chicago and in New York, and now at Stanford University, has drawn a great deal of attention nationally.[5] For a number of years Dr. Dement has worked with eye movements during sleep, as recorded by electro-encephalograms, in order to chart the pattern of dreams. He was experimenting particularly with the frequency of dreaming in subjects who were awakened whenever they started to dream when he discovered two things. Not only did these subjects who were deprived of their dreams step up the frequency of their attempts to dream, but if they continued to be cut off from completing their dreams, they soon began to show the signs of a nervous breakdown. As he deprived them of man's natural myth-making mechanism, the dream, these people became emotionally disturbed. Much of this work, it should be noted, has also been substantiated by the neuropsychiatric groups in various other universities.

Jung himself was a medical doctor and an empirical scientist. His books were intended for the medical profession, and he was very careful about the statements he made in them. Still he was accused by scientists of being mystical, and by religionists of reducing religion to a mental function. It has been very difficult to realize that he was simply describing the reality of the human psyche as he observed it. Jung, in fact, made very few metaphysical statements; he simply described what he discovered in his practice, in his travels, and in his study of mythology and related fields, one of the fields being the records of the medieval alchemists.

With an open-minded and objective view of human experience, he confirmed the discoveries of Freud that human motivation rises from a level of the psyche of which men are generally unconscious. Then, as he observed this, he began to see meanings within the deep or collective unconscious which are often superior to consciousness. In his own words:

> The assumption that the human psyche possesses layers that lie *below* consciousness is not likely to arouse serious opposition. But that there could just as well be layers lying *above* consciousness seems to be a surmise which borders on a *crimen laesae majestatis humanae* [high treason against human nature]. In my experience the conscious mind can only claim a relatively central position and must put up with the fact that the unconscious psyche transcends and as it were surrounds it on all sides. Unconscious contents connect it *backward* with physiological states on the one hand and archetypal data on the other. But it is

extended *forward* by intuitions which are conditioned partly by archetypes and partly by subliminal perceptions depending on the relativity of time and space in the unconscious.[6]

And the language the unconscious uses to express this superior wisdom, as well at its primitive or erotic material, is the mythological motif which appears in dreams and folk tales.

So far we have been talking in psychological terms. It must be noted, however, that Jung and Freud both believed that the unconscious, although nonmaterial, was real—very real. Probably this is seen most clearly in the fact that the unconscious can destroy a man's physical health and his emotional equilibrium. Thus, as soon as one identifies the realm of the collective unconscious with the realm of the spirit or with spiritual reality, then religion and mythology, far from being unimportant pastimes for children and dilettantes, become essential factors in human life. Jung did not suggest this identification in his published works until he came to write his profound and revealing autobiography, in which he set down his reflections as an old man; and this book, *Memories, Dreams, Reflections,* he directed was not to be published as part of his collected scientific works. But many of those who have understood Jung see that this identification is inevitable, and they believe that the religious use of myth becomes crucial in our time if man is to survive.

In his later years Jung's study and researches were directed almost entirely along these lines, rather than towards what is traditionally known as psychology. In certain ways, he might be thought of as an empirical theologian in this later work; even so, he remained empirical, describing experiences. In one of the late books he laid it on the line that people often rejected his ideas without examining the experiences on which they were based, and that whenever people had used his methods and discovered for themselves the experiences he described, the facts he gave about the unconscious had been confirmed. "One could see the moons of Jupiter even in Galileo's day," he added, "if one took the trouble to use his telescope."[7] I can heartily agree with Jung, since I have experienced many of these realities myself, and have also known many others who have done so.

At the end of his autobiography Jung wrote:

> I have, therefore, even hazarded the postulate that the phenomenon of archetypal configurations—which are psychic events *par excellence*—may be founded upon a *psychoid* base, that is, upon an only partially psychic and possibly altogether different form of being. For lack of empirical data I have neither knowledge nor understanding of such forms of being, which are commonly called spiritual. From the point of view of science, it is immaterial what I may *believe* on that score, and I must accept my ignorance. But insofar as the archetypes act upon me, they are real and actual to me, even though I do not know what their real nature is. . . . Nevertheless, we have good reason to suppose that behind this veil there exists the uncomprehended absolute object which affects and influences us—and to suppose it even, or particularly, in the case of psychic phenomena about which no verifiable statements can be made.[8]

Jung's religious attitude towards these realities, which are known largely through the dream and the myth, was stated even more definitely and clearly in a letter which he wrote to me in 1958:

> The real nature of the objects of human experience is still shrouded in darkness. The scientist can-

not concede a higher intelligence to Theology than to any other branch of human cognition. We know as little of a supreme being as of Matter. But there is as little doubt of the existence of a supreme being as of Matter. The world beyond is a reality, an experiential fact. We only don't understand it.

Rather, we "know." We know God, and we know a world beyond by experiencing it, and then we express our experiences in images, in myths. Conversely, as we come to understand and experience the myth, we are brought into contact with the realm of the nonphysical or that which religion speaks of as the realm of the spirit, and in doing so, we are dealing with realities, not just ideas or concepts. I can only repeat that I have experienced them and I know the reality of these things of which Jung speaks, of which mythology speaks. Psychology has tried to pin them down and understand them, but dealing with this realm of experience is a larger task than that.

By comparing two diagrams, one of the older view of the world, and the other of this new understanding based on man's experience, we can see something of the importance of this newer view for a religious approach to reality, and the need for myth in making the approach. The diagrams can only suggest what we are speaking about, but they do put some of the many factors into perspective, and hint at their relationship.

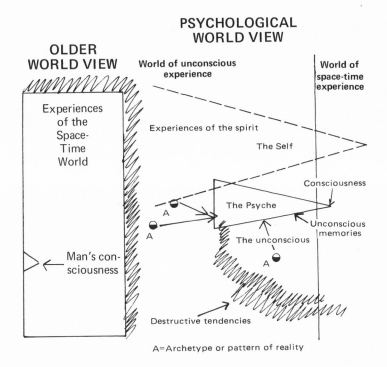

A=Archetype or pattern of reality

The diagram on the left represents the older world view of a space-time box as the only world that man knows, and which he learns about only through consciousness. In the newer view, the psyche itself is seen as extending into another realm of experience. This is shown in the second diagram by the small triangle in the center, with a world of experience striking it from each side. The outer world is there, and just as important to know. But through the unconscious psyche man can discover the Spirit, much as Jung described the transcendent "Self" (pictured by the open-ended, thus unlimited, triangle). The dark area below represents evil or destructive tendencies impinging on both the psyche and the outer world, while the small black and white globes suggest how the typical patterns of reality, or archetypes, are experienced. And for the most part, these experiences of the unconscious psyche can come to consciousness, where they can be understood and dealt with, only through myths and symbolic images.

Let us now summarize and come up with a definition of myth from the psychological framework of Jung. We will then be ready to see how Christians have understood and lived their central myth through most of the history of the church. Jung shows that:

1. There is a realm of objective nonphysical reality which we come to know through strange experiences of the psyche. We come to know this reality through the dream, the vision, the phantasy, the religious experience, the intuition and the myth.

2. Man cannot remain healthy if he is cut off from this realm of reality, which may be called either the collective unconscious or the realm of spirit. It is not the religious person, the person who uses myth and takes it seriously in ritual and understanding, who is either primitive or sick, but rather those who have lost their ability to use any myth and are thus cut off from their own unconscious depths.

3. It is the function of myth and ritual (the myth in action) to help men confront this realm of reality and deal creatively with it and find in this way direction towards greater maturity, wholeness and meaning.

4. The religious group which fails to use myth fails to make this connection and loses its essential reason for existence.

Myth then is a representation or a picturing of spiritual reality. Through images the myth provides an insight into the structure of this reality with its values and dangers and its direction and purpose, showing man how he can and must deal with it. Whenever any religious group is alive and vital, it will use mythological motifs to establish and offer this connection. Indeed I doubt if there is any other way to do it, and if the religious group fails to provide a way, this may become the task of the psychologist who is interested in providing emotional health to fill the gap left by religion.

I realized the importance of this kind of religion to Jung when I first talked with him, and happened to ask him which approach to the human psyche, and to healing its problems, was closest to his own. I expected to hear him mention some famous name or school of psychological therapy, but he named none of them. Instead, he answered: "The closest approach to my point of view was found among the classic Roman Catholic directors of conscience in France in the nineteenth century, among those men like Abbé Huvelin."

Perhaps the idea of knowledge coming to us in images still seems puzzling. It is well to remember that this approach to the nonphysical world is much the same as the way we actually know the physical world. So often we think that our sense experience of the world reveals it just as it is. Physics suggests, however, that instead of being substantial, the physical world is a whirling mass of particles so tiny that it is even difficult to imagine how they could combine to make a smooth, hard table-top, or a rain cloud. Our sense experience has to be supplemented by all kinds of images and formulas to tell us much about the outer world, just as we learn something about the nonphysical one from mythical images tested out in experience. Arthur Eddington has discussed at length the strange way that man receives his knowledge of the physical world in *Science and the Unseen World*. Mythological thinking is not as strange as some people think once they begin to see the total universe as it is.

VIII
Religion
and Myth

It is odd that the church is so slow to take advantage of the new appreciation of myth and mythological thinking. This would seem to be a natural. But there are reasons for the reluctance. The church's fear of scientific thinking keeps it from realizing the latest developments in physics, evolutionary thought, medicine and psychiatry. In addition the rational set of mind has such a hold on most academic Christians—who have something to say about the theology of the rest of us—that they simply do not hear what is said when any other meaning is expressed, any meaning that cannot be understood rationally.

This is a troubling situation because it has cut so many Christians off from the vitality of religious experience and myth as well as the church's rituals. Where religion has been vital, not only have the value and function of myth and ritual been emphasized, but there has also been emphasis on the dream, the vision, and spiritual intuitions which, as we have suggested, are all of one piece with the myth. Although Western Christianity has shown no concern with these experiences in recent times, we find that nearly all religions have considered them the way *par excellence* by which God reveals himself to man. We find the same tradition in the Bible and in Greek literature. We also find the same tradition among the sophisticated philosophers of the church during the early years of its life.

These were the men, men of great ability and stature, who laid the foundations of Christianity. Irenaeus, Justin Martyr, the great Origen of Alexandria, Tertullian, Cyprian, Athanasius, Basil, Augustine, Chrysostom, were all men of unusual, even gigantic minds, and yet most of us are actually ignorant of their work.[1] Their thinking presents a world view which has been forgotten today, even though Christianity would probably have been lost without their careful thought. The reason, in large part, that we know so little of that thinking is that it touches areas which lie outside the spotlight of rational materialism. Instead, it looks at the world mythologically.

All of these men realized the value of dreams and visions. They were aware that spiritual reality often speaks through these manifestations of the nonrational side of man. They also knew and valued the Biblical story, not only as it had happened so many years before, but as it played upon men's lives in their own time. Because they understood this and were able to express it mythologically, these men were able to tap the power that made Christian belief the moving force in the lives of so many people at that time. They became the great leaders that they were because they allowed the Christian myth to act fully and freely in their own lives.

Basil, for instance, had to fight almost single-handed to keep the Christian faith from being watered down by one-sided thinking, by men who wanted to explain Christian experience more rationally. At the height of his dispute with the Roman Emperor Valens, Basil was about to be punished and exiled. The preparations to seize him were all but complete when friends of the emperor came to tell him that Valens' little son was dangerously ill. They expected to have to plead with him to come and offer healing. But Basil did not stop to think of his own safety. He went immediately to the palace and was taken to the child's bedside, where he laid his hands on the boy and prayed. Those who were present described the power that was felt, and how the child's condition improved from that moment.[2] Because Basil knew the reality described by the Christian story, he was able to allow the power of God to work in his life without fear.

The same power was seen in the life of Ambrose when, as head of the Western church, he had to face Theodosius after the emperor had caused a slaughter of innocent citizens over the murder of one imperial officer. Because Ambrose understood how God can speak in a dream, and listened, he was able to take a firm stand. And later, looking back on what had happened, he could say:

> I have loved a man who esteemed a reprover more than a flatterer. He threw on the ground all the royal attire that he was wearing. He wept publicly in church for his sin. . . . I have loved a man who in his dying hour kept asking for me. . . .[3]

It was the same power, expressed in much the same way, that made Augustine's conversion possible, and enabled John Chrysostom to draw his congregations to him in exile. The same power sustained Christians from Justin Martyr on so that they could face suffering and death victoriously, and even pray for their persecutors. These were men who convinced a whole world of the reality of their experience.

They understood the stories in the Bible and passed on that understanding in volume after volume of their writings. The mythological character of their understanding of the fall, of the nature of evil, about human destiny, prophecy, angels and demons, about the death and resurrection of Jesus, is evident on nearly every page. The present devaluation of mythology and the dream in our Western Christian church is completely foreign to the thinking and writing of those incomparable first Christians, who made what they knew stick in spite of persecution and criticism. The fact that we are "Christian" today is the evidence. These men founded our Trinitarian faith and fought for it. In my opinion the disappearance of mythological thinking in the church is a sign of its departure from its religious roots.

There is one branch of Christianity which has not been touched by this devaluation. The Eastern or Greek Orthodox tradition has never turned its back upon the dream or the myth. In its rich and full liturgy, in its icons and stories, it has continued to believe that spiritual reality is mediated to men through mythological images in story and actions, and in the pictorial representation of the icon. Those who know something of the Greek church and its depth and richness will realize that in it the Christian myth (and remember once again that *myth* is not a word which distinguishes between historical fact and unrealized imagination) is still richly portrayed and lived out. The whole mythology of the angelic and the demonic is very much alive there, as in the Greek monasteries where monks are called to the angelic state and wear a habit which they know as the "angel's robes."

Perhaps a brief explanation of how the Western church came to devalue mythology will be helpful in understanding the position of Western man at the present time and why he turns to the myths of Siberia or of ancient India rather than to a living religious myth of his own. Until the eleventh century, when the thinking of Aristotle reached Western Europe, men had believed along with Plato that man had three ways of knowing:

1. He knew by sense experience.

2. He knew by reason.

3. And he knew by what Plato called Divine madness, or a direct contact with nonphysical reality; myths were one result of this last kind of knowing.

The Importance of Aristotle

But according to Aristotle, who tried to establish his own position in contrast to Plato, men gain knowledge only by their sense experience and their reason working upon it; they have no direct contact with spiritual reality (or the unconscious as modern psychology has called it), and so no need for myths. Thus, we find little mythological thinking in Aristotle, nor any real effort to show its value. Although underneath he knew better than to deny the value of myth completely, and even affirmed it privately before his death,[4] his interest lay in the material world and understanding it rationally.

Aristotle had not been popular in the ancient world, but his ideas were picked up by the materialistically-minded Arabs as they were developing their culture, and from there his works were introduced into Western Europe. They became the rage, stimulating a whole intellectual revival. It soon became necessary for the church to deal with this point of view, and through the genius of Thomas Aquinas all of church ideas were rewritten within the framework of Aristotle's ideas with their mythological character reduced to a bare minimum.

Aquinas became the basic theological authority for the Roman Catholic church, and he has had a deep influence on almost all modern Protestant theology. Thus, mythology was torn out by the roots in Western Christianity. This was not so important for Catholicism until recent years. Since the Roman Church continued to emphasize the mythological actions of the Mass, demanding attendance at this service for all of its members, Roman Catholics are steeped in mythology whether they know it or not. There has also been an interest in shrines and relics and rituals like the Stations of the Cross. The practice of praying in images has also been kept alive by Ignatian prayer. As one astute Catholic friend of mine has commented, "The Catholic Church has an Aristotelian head and a Platonic heart, and it has usually listened to its heart more than its head. This is the reason that it has stayed alive."

Western Protestantism did not have these unbroken traditions to support it. Instead the ideas of Aristotle were accepted as the sole basis for belief and so it remained, thus cutting the Protestant off from his mythological roots. Protestants have tried to make their religion completely logical and sensible, and also in impeccable taste. They have accepted Aristotle and his world view without ever thinking about it or without realizing that there was any other point of view and have done so with annihilating consistency. The result is that the average Western Protestant, completely cut off from his own myth, turns to the Vedas or theosophy, to Masonry, or to a struggle for power, or even war, to give him mythological symbols which his faith does not encompass. His religion has become merely a logical and rational process. Even emotion is suspect in most Protestant circles. Calvin put it very clearly when he said that "corporeal images are unworthy of the majesty of God, and they diminish reverence and increase error," and that "everything respecting God which is learned from images is futile and false."[5]

This attitude makes it impossible for most modern Protestantism to appreciate the mythological content of Christianity. If no knowledge of the spiritual realm can come through images, then all mythology is futile, vain, and leads one astray. The same can be said of visions and dreams. One can begin to understand that it is not only the scientific world which rejected the value of the myth. Even the church, which in ages past was custodian of man's myths, has turned its back upon myth, has forgotten its meaning, and has lost the ability to interpret and use it.

The final result of this rejection is found in the book *Honest to God* by Bishop John Robinson. Since mythology no longer makes sense to modern man, the Bishop concludes, therefore it must all be cut out from the Christian faith and practice. According to Robinson there is nothing that man can do to change things. Man is simply conditioned to his present point of view and must accept it as inevitable. Robinson has taken his assumption from Rudolf Bultmann and the existential philosophers, who simply take it for granted that there is only one route for man to follow.

Unfortunately the same attack has now been made upon the whole Roman Catholic position, in a way far more devastating even than Robinson's sincere attempt to rescue some hope for belief out of the shreds of a Gospel without myth. This book, *Jesus: Son of Man, (Jesus: Menschensohn)* which was on the bestseller lists for months in Germany, was written by Rudolf Augstein, the editor of *Der Spiegel* (the German version of *Time Magazine* or *Newsweek*). While it offers nothing that has not been said a dozen times over, this book has struck home. The author was trained by the Jesuit order, and he combines Jesuit scholarship with breezy slang in a thoroughgoing effort to show that the church has no right to base any kind of teaching, informative or authoritative, on the life of Jesus. He protests that Jesus of Nazareth never existed as a conscious messiah or savior, and that the church has long known this and yet has presumed to tell men what to do. He suggests that Bultmann is the best example of sincere Christian futility, because he has not yet admitted that man will have to get along without religion.

From this point of view, myth is merely man's attempt to explain things that happen to him and what exists in the universe without using logical concepts. Myth was a primitive method of expression which was no longer necessary as soon as men became able to use logic and science. For sensible modern man it is quite incomprehensible. And therefore according to this point of view what is needed is a new and rational method of expressing the essence of the Gospel message. The task of modern Christianity is to tailor the Gospel to suit people today, who are accustomed to using logical steps in getting what they want. And so a belief has grown that new thought forms, new rational and historical formulations are required to make the Christian message relevant to the modern world.

This view assumes, without investigating any further, that the nineteenth century scientific way of looking at life, based on the position of Aristotle and Aquinas, is the only adequate outlook on life. If this is indeed the only adequate way of explaining and experiencing life, then Bultmann, Robinson, and also Bonhoeffer and Paul Tillich (as he expresses himself in his *Systematic Theology*) * are quite correct and the Christian faith must be completely recast. It is doubtful, if this is done, that much of the essence or power of that faith can be retained, or in fact that anything will remain of Christianity. It is not easy, if it is possible at all, to reconcile the gospel message with the positivistic thought which we have inherited from Aristotle. If this is the only point of view from which to look at life, then the concern, almost the terror, with which these men grapple with Christianity is understandable.

There is no argument about the way modern Western man *does* look at the world. He already sees it only from this point of view, and this is a very real problem. We have reason for concern if the chances are that the ideas of Aristotle and the positivists are right. Is it any wonder that the pentecostal and conservative evangelical movements have grown like a floodtide in our day? There is

---

*Two points of view are found in Tillich. This one is presented in the first two volumes of his *Systematic Theology*, while in the last volume of that major work and in many of his sermons and other writings there is a more mystical element. He never brought the two together.

need for action to maintain something of the Christian faith. But we have two very different problems to deal with here. It is one thing to be afraid that Aristotelian positivism might be true, and quite another to assume that this is so simply because it is the current accepted idea. There is evidence for a different point of view, one which has been supported by the philosophy of Plato, by Christianity in its vital years, and in modern times by Jung, Heisenberg, Gödel, Teilhard de Chardin, and many others. Just where does the real problem lie?

A Different World View

What the evidence actually suggests is that the fault lies, not in the mythological images, but rather within man himself. And what we are suggesting is that the problem is not to rework or restate the gospel message, or to create new thought forms or to create new images. The problem, instead, is to awaken modern man from his hidden assumptions and give him a chance to think mythologically again. Largely through the efforts of Aquinas, modern man is like one who has been stuffed into a box which gives him no outlook, no idea that any reality exists outside his cubbyhole. Far from having outgrown his need for mythological thinking, man needs this ability more than ever today, because myth can act almost like throwing open a window to reveal reality that is not being touched by the rational, Aristotelian approach.

Getting at the essence of the Gospel rationally only deepens the problem. The New Testament is talking about things that really happened or realities; it does not talk about distilled essences. And the only way that rational thought can deal with these realities is to lift them out of their living environment and prepare a slice for microscopic examination. Mythology on the other hand, can work with them as they are and live, as they merge and change in their original context. The psyche of man can understand such contents because myth uses images and symbols which arise from this same depth. John Sanford's *The Kingdom Within* shows how powerfully and yet simply the sayings of Jesus portray this relationship. We need more books like this one to help us grasp the deep meaning and wisdom of Jesus in approaching the psyche (or soul).

Thus the problem confronting the modern church is not so much to adapt to modern thought forms, but to discover this new, and yet very old way of looking at reality mythologically. This is the Platonic, the psychological, the Christian way of expressing spiritual reality, through images and symbols, and it is the only way of approaching this realm as a living reality. Otherwise it must be broken down into elements and is dead. Can you imagine expressing appreciation for a good dinner of lobster and cherries jubilee by talking about the chemical elements that constituted it? That would be very much like religion without myth.

Religion which deals with these living spiritual realities is a very practical matter. Theology may be theoretical but, as we have discussed, religion is practical in essence. It has the task of relating man to the spiritual realm without danger, or at least with lessened danger. Since there is the close tie between the spiritual realm and the unconscious which we have already described, we can see that an individual who is flooded by spiritual reality may be so swept off his feet that he loses his bearings in the outer physical world. He can become mentally ill. By being drowned in the unconscious, or in the nonphysical reality that surrounds us, or the spiritual world—call it what you wish—he can lose touch with physical reality, the reality which we Westerners value so much. *This*

realm of the collective unconscious or spiritual reality is
a dynamic realm and is not to be played around with.

Real religion, in fact, is always dangerous business,
but through its mythology religion can give man an entrance to this realm, or contact with it, with a measure
of safety. Myth and ritual act as transformers in bringing
people the value of spiritual reality, just as an electrical
transformer turns high voltage into usable current which
can cook meals and light houses. The dream also provides
the same kind of stepped-down encounter. A naked encounter with the spiritual forces that surround us is so
dangerous that only a few heroic souls can withstand its
power. Ideally the task of the priest is to be the one who
makes this contact and then mediates that experience to
others. This is not very different from the way the scientist mediates his laboratory contact with atoms and physical forces in the form of drugs and other products and
techniques which we can use. And the language and techniques that are used in the priestly mediation are mainly
those of mythology.

The basic task of all religion is to help men to become
conscious of spiritual reality, to confront it and to be
transformed by it. Psychologically this can be described
as helping man—in the first stage—to be conscious, to
become free from his identification with the collective
unconscious, to help him achieve his own identity and
find his own individual destiny. This is no easy task; it is
the way of the hero. As Joseph Campbell shows so clearly
in *The Hero With a Thousand Faces,* this figure who
"ventures forth from the world of common day into a
region of supernatural wonder"[6] is a mythological expression common to the religions of all peoples. The first task
of the hero is to free himself from the old attitudes and
start on his quest.

The second stage of the religious way compares psychologically with facing the darkness and the shadow with-

in the individual, or dealing with the native or primitive side of the unconscious. In its mythological motif, the hero deals with the inner adversary in the form of a dragon, the medusa, the many-headed monster, or in the form of the pharisee within. While help may be given once this side of the personality is faced, this is still difficult; there is no painless way of coming into contact with spiritual reality. John Sanford shows how much emphasis Jesus placed on this aspect of the religious process in his teachings about the kingdom of God. Sometimes the religious quest begins with immersion in this darkness. Then the task is the struggle to find some light.

The last stage of the religious way is that of transformation, in which the divine element—the self, as Jung calls it —breaks through and gives more than ordinary insight and power, the confidence, vision and understanding which have been the possession of all really mature religious people. This is symbolized in myth by receiving the golden fleece, or the treasure which lies under the dragon, or in Christian terms as finding the Holy Grail, receiving the Holy Ghost, or being filled with the Holy Spirit. The Christian who comes to this experience is then expected to carry this power on to fight the spiritual forces of darkness and unconsciousness which he meets in the world.

Religious practice provides three approaches to this way, three mythological methods of coming to terms with spiritual reality and finding the treasure within it. One way is to study the myth in its historical context, to read the religious texts and the lives and writings of the great religious leaders, like the Bible and the many writings of the fathers of the church. And for modern Christians this means trying to see the psychological meaning of myth in the development of human consciousness. A second way is through ritual in which the mythological story is acted out and the believer participates in the myth through his action, in services like the Mass, baptism, or group prayer.

And third, he can sometimes step into the myth imaginatively through meditation, actually entering the spiritual world himself and becoming active and effective in it.

Before we go on to consider these methods in practice, and how they can touch our own lives and make this Christian myth of ours effective in today's world, let us try to understand the reality of this world view I am proposing. And then let us see whether or not this view tallies with the Christian approach offered by Jesus of Nazareth.

The Reality of Spirit

If men are to deal with the whole of reality, and not just fool themselves by thinking they are doing the best job they can with the world as it is, then men will have to make their peace with spiritual reality as well as with the physical world. In fact, as we have tried to suggest in other ways, the most important action man can undertake is to face or confront and come to terms with the world of spirit. Once man begins to get his balance among these realities—to know himself and his relation to that world—then he will find his way in the outer world far clearer and without so many roadblocks. Knowing that one is doing his level best to face up to these controlling realities which can be both good and evil, he will find far fewer experiences that are insurmountable and throw him entirely for a loss. Or, as Jesus remarked towards the end of his sermon on the mount, "Set your mind on God's kingdom and his justice before everything else, and all the rest will come to you as well."

Yet our modern world did not stop to look at these realities within man himself until a handful of medical men found they had no other choice if they wanted to help their patients get well. Even then, it took quite a while for the realization to grow that realities of a basically religious nature were involved. The church had long before lost its interest in any reality that was purely psychic in form. And so, in order to help people who had been left without any effective grasp on these realities, medicine was forced into this area which the church once handled, but had lately abdicated. These men believed that the only way to get at the serious problems of their patients, from sexual maladjustment to violence and even psychosomatic disease, was to work with these spiritual or psychic realities.

One of the primary functions of the church and religion has been to deal with realities of that nature, and Dr. Jung himself once remarked to me that he had looked around for clergy who understood such things; but he had found so few to whom he could refer his patients with this kind of need that he was forced to learn to work with these spiritual realities as best he could. He believed that some neuroses, particularly those involving loss of meaning, could and should be handled by religious professionals who were properly trained. In the early years of Christianity the church was known as the place to bring those who were sick, either mentally or physically, and there are many records of healing found in the best sources. A vital Christianity still has this power.

From a psychological point of view these psychic realities have been treated almost like a new discovery. The psychologists recognize these recurring forms of psychic reality—which can be pinned down and classified—and call them complexes, autonomous complexes, or archetypes. The New Testament and the fathers of the church called them spirits, angels (although psychologists have not always recognized that a complex could have a creative and useful aspect) , and demons. Both sets of names indicate realities which have a life of their own, and appear to operate independently of the conscious human psyche.

The psychologist defines and describes what he sees in the psyche empirically and tentatively, while theology, when it believes in them, describes and defines these realities metaphysically and ontologically. Both are looking towards the same experience, and occasionally they admit the validity of the other's description. The psychologist sometimes speaks of the substantive reality of autonomous complexes, and the theologian, if not totally rationalistic, at times admits the psychological effect of spiritual realities. In fact, one of the men who has written with depth and clarity comparing the two approaches was the Catholic theologian, Fr. Victor White, who was well versed in psychology. His book, *God and the Unconscious,* is one of the best in this area.

Psychologists and theologians both agree in describing two important characteristics of these realities. Psychologically and spiritually, whether one calls them complexes or spiritual beings, they can be either upbuilding, creative forces, or negative and destructive influences. From the New Testament on, the great Christian writers who dealt with the world of spirit in depth have stressed its negative as well as its positive side, and this is equally true of writers who discuss the unconscious and its complexes. The belief that anything which is "spiritual" must be *ipso facto* "good" is just as naive as the feeling that everything "psychological" is "bad," or at least a little naughty.

The other attribute on which there is agreement is the effect these realities have upon human life. One may start, for instance, with Paul's instructions to the Ephesians to put on the whole armor of God against the superhuman forces, "the Powers who originate the darkness in this world," or on the other hand with Freud's vivid descriptions of actual experiences in *Studies in Hysteria.* Neither literature will leave one exactly complacent, with their descriptions of how nonmaterial realities can and do possess and control human lives. Psychological complexes or angelic-demonic beings, whatever name they are called by, do have direct contact with the human psyche. They can determine the quality and direction of a man's life, controlling his energy, his actions, and his influence in the physical world, while he as an individual is practically powerless before them. He may even wish to act very differently and still be unable to change, no matter how hard he tries.

Obviously there is a relation between this power which can control the individual and the qualities of good and evil in nonphysical reality. This has been demonstrated psychologically by careful studies of men like Hitler and Goethe, while the same story has been told in symbolic terms by C. S. Lewis and Charles Williams and other imaginative writers. Probably the most telling modern descriptions of these two attributes of nonphysical reality are found in the chilling novels of Charles Williams and the phantasies of J.R.R. Tolkien, who both depict with terrifying clarity the negative side of spiritual reality and its boundless influence over men's lives.

If these beings did not have such power over human life, they would hardly be worth so much discussion. They might attract the attention of a few remote philosophers,* and that would be all. Instead, anyone who attempts to help human beings direct their lives soon finds how practical it is to consider these realities. Most men seem to be in the grip of forces they cannot consciously control. It is not only a Nietzsche, a Melville or a Virginia Woolf (whom we shall discuss later on), but most of the rest of us who are caught, unsuspecting, by the power of spiritual reality

---

*Angels certainly attracted the attention of Aquinas, who was known as "the angelic doctor" because of his lengthy discussions of them. Aquinas, however, did not believe that the angelic and the demonic could have any direct influence upon the human psyche. Following Aristotle, he feared that admitting such influence would rob man of his moral capacity, his freedom. But would it not be more true to say that man has been given the task of recognizing how unfree he is, and then of trying through Christ to become more free?

which can destroy as well as create. Almost any reality which we fail to confront and deal with in some way, will try to possess us. This is as true of autonomous complexes or spirits as of germs and bacteria.

Not only do these forces touch individual lives, but they can reach into history, and break forth into actual physical reality in a whole mythological pattern. They can weave together many lives and events so that a whole myth becomes repeated in history; by this we mean that the drama between archetypal or angel-demon powers is then transferred from the individual imagination and struggle to actual outer events. In one case a whole people became mobilized for war and set out under the banner of the god, Wotan, to conquer the world. Again, men dreamed for centuries about the dying and rising god before the myth was actualized in history. They had also observed how often the forces of destruction are let loose upon a creative and victorious man. The power which enables men to be great has a negative side, and the greater the man, the more subject he is to the ravaging effects of the negative side of this reality.

The ancients pictured this aspect of spiritual reality as the negative side of the great mother archetype which, like the spider, gives birth and then destroys.* In one myth, Innana gives her creative love to Tammuz, the young ruler; in another myth Adonis is loved by the great mother Aphrodite, or Attis by Cybele, and then the victorious young hero is destroyed, seized by the underworld, or gored by the wild boar, or maimed by his own hand. Again and again his fate is determined by the dark and negative side of the goddess. This mother, it is true, raises

---

*Among the same peoples there were other myths, of course, portraying the destructive forces of spiritual reality. The image of the dying and rising god happened to be the one that worked in people's imagination, undoubtedly because it represented most accurately the realities they found within their psyches.

her beloved from his death, but she cannot offer him eternal life. The evil follows the good and death again follows the resurrection in endless cycle. In the myths of other non-Christian peoples the same power of evil is pictured. There is no exit, no way off the teeter-totter, because to these non-Christians spiritual reality is amoral and the unconscious itself has no way of making a choice between the positive and the negative.

History shows almost precise examples of this mythological pattern. The young Alexander falls ill with a fever and dies in his thirty-third year. Caesar in his moment of triumph is struck down by Brutus. Lincoln is shot by the actor who even saw himself fulfilling the role of a new Brutus. All of us recall vividly the archetypal pattern of Kennedy's death which we have already described. And yet we have still thought of these as simply chance events, tied to deeper reality only by some historian's facile way with facts.

How seldom do we look at the mythological pattern as it moves deep within the lives of individuals, prompting them to meet fate, to meet events following almost exactly the meaning outlined by the myth. Yet most of us experienced this meaning in the assassination of John Kennedy; many people were touched at a deeper level of their lives than they knew they possessed. I had knowledge myself at the time of a number of people who were experiencing almost more than they were able to handle, far more in fact than the political and business fears they felt. One of these individuals was almost swept into mental illness so deeply did the archetypal significance of Kennedy's death strike him.

The Power of Christ

The death of Jesus on Golgotha was an expression of

this same archetypal pattern, of the same amorality of spiritual forces working itself out in history. The creative, healing and concerned man of spirit was struck down. The greatest of shamans was destroyed. But this time the outcome was quite different. The destructive side of spiritual reality seemed to conquer, but then it was turned back in the resurrection. The negative side did not remain victorious or triumphant. Once the events of Holy Week are seen as the manifestation of the negative side of spiritual reality —archetypal and mythological reality operating through men—then the resurrection can be seen as the overwhelmingly important event which it was. It can be seen as the defeat of negative spiritual powers, rather than just an interesting historical accident.

Easter was the day on which these negative forces were defeated and chained. Jesus had submitted to the powers of destructiveness which were unleashed through Judas, Caiaphas, the Sanhedrin, Pilate, and the Roman army; historically their actions were then entirely nullified. But this was only a part of what actually happened. The reality which Jesus met on Golgotha went far beyond the group of men and their personal responsibility for his death. These, in fact, were far from being evil men bent on harm; probably they were bent only on what they thought was right, without being aware of anything else. And from the unconscious a deeper, archetypal power took over. Mythologically the wild boar was manifested. The Evil One had his way. This was the reality which Jesus knew and faced, and through him the mythological pattern of destructiveness was brought to a grinding halt.

By his resurrection a change was made in the spiritual constitution of reality so that the hopes of men were realized. This was the hope for victory over the negative side of the great mother archetype, victory over the dark and destructive shadow of their own unconsciousness, or victory over the Evil One himself. In this way the very nature of nonphysical reality was changed; the negative side of these powers lost their freedom. A battle took place in the mythological realm of spiritual reality. The Christ was victorious. And spiritual evil, the mythological wild boar, was put in chains, no longer free.

The image which the early church used most frequently was of Jesus paying a ransom for the release of prisoners; through his death and resurrection mankind was ransomed from the power of evil. As Gustav Aulén has shown in *Christus Victor,* this understanding was practically universal for over a thousand years, from New Testament days until the time of Anselm. The church understood the crucifixion and resurrection, not just as a single action taken by God in the first century A.D., but as the continuing rescue of man from the power of the Evil One.

Of course this is difficult to believe if one doubts that reality has a negative side. But with more and more evil wandering around loose today, how can we push it aside just to keep our metaphysics tidy and rational? I am reminded of Berdyaev's remark as he reflected back over the Russian revolution, that whatever else appeared, one could observe that evil seemed to be both clever and pervasive. If one observes the actual record of experience, and not through the rose-colored glasses of rationality, it certainly appears that there is something quite real operating in opposition to the creative influences in the universe. When one is hurt himself, it is real enough. Yet how often do we stop to ask if there might be something equally real to the mythological idea that Christ saves man through His defeat of evil?

Let's put the elements of this idea, which is classically known as the atonement, into the same diagram we have used to outline man's psychological experiences on page 119, sketching out the same things that he experiences with their theological, rather than psychological, names.

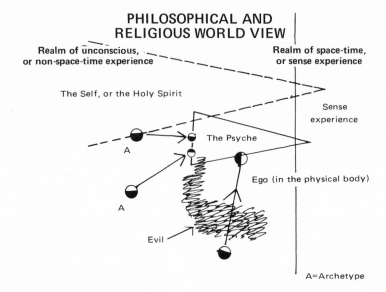

PHILOSOPHICAL AND
RELIGIOUS WORLD VIEW

Realm of unconscious,
or non-space-time experience

Realm of space-time,
or sense experience

The Self, or the Holy Spirit

Sense
experience

The Psyche

A

Ego (in the physical body)

A

Evil

A=Archetype

Using this sketch to represent the incarnation, the central triangle stands for the *soul* of the man Jesus Christ, overshadowed by the *Holy Spirit* (to use a good Biblical term), suggested by the open-ended triangle. *Evil* (the dark area below), with a foothold in both man's soul and the outer world, is first pushed back and then counterattacks. Jesus faces evil—temptation in the wilderness, attacks by the scribes and Pharisees, the bloody sweat and agony of Gethsemane, and finally betrayal, condemnation, and crucifixion. Then in the resurrection the Holy Spirit completely surrounds him, breaking the grasp of evil on man's soul entirely. From then on any man can share in this pattern. Whenever someone accepts the indwelling Spirit of Christ and is willing to feel the meaning of His suffering for man's sake, the power and destructiveness of evil are pushed back once more. The Holy Spirit moves closer to that man, and through him to others, and thus evil must release its hold.

Is there a way of explaining how this was done? Why was Jesus the one chosen by destiny for the task? Although these are very difficult questions, we should try to understand the events as best we can. Jesus is described as the Son of God, and this is a reality which can best be understood in mythological terms. Both in his actions and in his conscious awareness he united the father principle with the creative aspects of the great mother. In him consciousness and unconsciousness were brought into union; the consciousness and righteousness of Jahweh, the Jewish father God, were joined with the warmth and kindness and concern of the ancient mother goddesses.

Here was the one who was perfectly whole, a union of the opposites, one who could deal with any aspect of archetypal or spiritual reality, and so he rose victorious from the death that those powers inflicted upon him. Since Jesus was neither a tool of the amoral great mother nor only an instrument of the cold and harsh father God, he was not subject to the negative side of either one. Because he was whole, he was able to defeat evil which is always only partial. Being conscious, he could conquer evil which springs out of unconsciousness. His wholeness, combining the reality of the earthly Mary and the spiritual Jahweh, was victorious over unconsciousness and evil. It is not possible to say much more than this.

The most important result, however, can be known in our own lives. The victory which Jesus won over these forces can actually be ours, for in the unconscious and in the spiritual realm there is no time and no space. The victory is only waiting for us to accept and use it, by learning to make our own struggle with the forces of unconsciousness and evil. This is the basic belief which the early church demonstrated in action: What was accomplished there was done once and for all and has continuing significance for men who become conscious of it. Mythologically the Gorgon's heads, the devastating floods, the wild boar, which still paralyze and destroy and ravage lives from the unconscious of men, have been defeated. And these are forces which must be defeated if men are not always to remain pawns in their hands.

This is the message of Easter and the resurrection—that men who learn how to come to the victorious Christ find that they are led through this territory of dark spiritual realities to victory in spite of every affliction. If this is true, and men can share in the same victory which Christ won over the forces of evil and darkness, then it is of the greatest importance to find this reality. How can we seek it as a practical part of our lives, appropriating it for ourselves and for those around us? Let us look at three basic ways in which we can grasp this victory—in action, in thought, and in imagination.

IX

Sharing in the Victory:
The Practice of Prayer

Christians can talk and preach until doomsday about the great victory which is available to all of us, but unless there is some way in which the ordinary individual can seize that victory for his own life, the whole Christian story becomes a tantalizing frustration. One might as well be offered a million dollars on condition that he leave it in the bank and not touch it, receive interest from it or borrow on it in this lifetime; it would do him about as much good. In fact, it is almost worse to see the possibility of a real victory over evil, and then find no way of getting to it, than to believe that there is no hope and that one must grin and bear life stoically. Christianity is then no longer a living myth, but dead history along with all the other futile attempts to conquer the world by heroic words and deeds.

There are two processes which Christians have believed give men access to this victory, to the unsearchable riches of Christ that come with it. These are prayer and meditation, neither of which is exactly unknown today. But one problem with them today is that we have thought of prayer only in terms of an intellectual and rational process, and we have often dismissed meditation because it could not be made to fit with this idea of practical usefulness. Yet few people have found the victory I have been talking about by using only their rational and logical mental processes.

Real prayer seems to be a living process combining, first, a real conviction about the spiritual world and the realities in it; second, the courage to act and to continue to act; and third, the use of imaginative meditation. Each one of these practices makes the others more real. This is a spiral process in which one discovers more about each as he ascends the spiral. Without conviction the other two become lifeless. Without action neither of the others remains rooted in the reality of life. Without meditation there is no opening through which the richness and reality of the spiritual world can pour out into the other activities.

We separate these three aspects of a genuine religious life, one of which is a living prayer, only for analysis to help the individual learn to use all three. We shall spend most of our time and effort describing imaginative meditation because it is so little known today and so little understood as a part of the customary religious practice of today. Again, all three are necessary for mature religious life and experience. Why is it so difficult for human beings to realize that there can be several essential elements in one process?

Action and Conviction

Without some kind of outer action the religious process becomes almost entirely internal, spiritual, psychic and gnostic. It becomes pietistic in the worst sense, because it is unrelated to the world. The most startling thing about Christianity is that the Spirit became incarnate; it entered physical reality, joined with flesh. Christianity is the most materialistic and practical of man's major religions. It has never considered the material world evil in the sense that the Gnostics did. And what a man does in the outer physical world indicates his real belief far better than what he *thinks* he believes. One may have the most carefully defined doctrine of the Trinity, and turn it into an actual spiritual liability by failing to act so that his life manifests the reality of spirit and the power of love which Jesus asked of his followers. I am not saying that belief is *un*important, but I am saying that trying to believe in a vacuum is not only meaningless but is downright dangerous.

When one says his prayers and goes to church—even when he is doing better at cursing God than praising Him —when he reads the Gospel narrative of Jesus and takes part in communion, when he tries to act the way of love and gives his tithe faithfully, then the reality of this victory begins to take place in an actual life. That person may still be muttering under his breath, "Lord, I believe; help thou mine unbelief!" at the very time he is acting faithfully. Faith comes as a result of action; it is a gift, but a gift which is seldom given to those who do not open their lives by action. Those who do have this kind of acted-upon faith in Christ's victory find, usually to their astonishment, that they are sharing in its results.

How seldom do we take Jesus Christ seriously. He tells us that we are entertaining Him in our lives when we minister to the hungry, the naked, the imprisoned. And sometimes we do show love to these people, and then turn right around and cut it off from those closest to us. Again, it is not a matter of either/or, but of both/and. If we are to love others as He has loved us (a rather radical commandment, but the only really new one that He gave), it takes some real action, yes, social action, action toward helping other human beings and some real determination. Still, if we really believe that Christ, through his love, routed the forces of evil so that we could be ransomed from them, and then we don't even try to follow His way, we come close to losing ourselves in hypocrisy.

What does this love mean? It means first of all considering the idea that, as His followers, our task is to live out love. Then it means carrying this idea out in action. It means listening to others without judging or criticizing them, because one cannot even begin to love a person until he has at least listened and tried to find out what the other person is like. Love is not just a warm feeling towards another human being; rather, it is making the other person feel loved himself, and this is impossible without listening. It also means trying to love one's self, the most difficult of all tasks because—when we stop to think—we have the whole story on ourselves. This is one reason so few of us even try to love ourselves, and it is then impossible to love others, because we are busy projecting onto them the parts of ourselves which we cannot stand. Whenever one cannot stand some characteristic in other people, it means that that characteristic is probably unconsciously part of himself and he has not looked at it.

After this beginning, there is the task of loving one's family, even when we come home from a hard day's work and the children are obnoxious. Convincing one's spouse of his love, once all his weaknesses and faults have been exposed, can be a most difficult task even when there is time enough to do this day after day. The garden variety family expends little Christian love on each other, particularly when their college-age son comes home with long hair, or a daughter gets pregnant out of wedlock, or the last teen-ager starts using pot. But the least we can do is to show love within the family, or within the religious community, no matter how difficult or peculiar the members. Loving under these circumstances underscores our belief in the Trinity, since it means living out this idea that God who is love became incarnate in Jesus Christ and gives the same spirit to those who wish to grow in spirit and truth.

Then there are the numbers of people to whom one

knows he should express love in some way, people like the harried clerk in a store, the crotchety next-door neighbor, one's fellow workmen or even one's employer (*or* employees). And there is one real way to show love here, to be a Trinitarian, atonement-centered Christian. This is to give the other person room to live, in other words for one to create the conditions in which the other person can grow to the maximum of his ability, as his own circumstances permit. We may not even be required to act, but only to keep from disapproving or interfering. Again there are the strangers, those who are not at home in the clique, the newcomers at church, for instance. These people have a claim on us as brothers, and we are asked to show them friendliness. And finally, there are one's enemies. Jesus was very specific about this: we are to love or care for and do good to the people we dislike, and to those who dislike us.

This is putting one's faith into action. It also involves the whole area of social action, which means getting at and reforming the structures in society that keep men from growing. Unless prayer is supported by this kind of action, it is not likely to bring forth many good fruits. Again, this is only a part of such action. One also needs times of quiet and reflection. One needs time to look over one's life and see how he is doing and to check on his angers and fears and how to figure out a method of handling them. These are only suggestions that need to be spelled out and thought about, and they are ones which could take a whole book, one that has been on my mind for a long time.

In addition to this, there are times when action must be supported by good, solid thought, and for some people this is very important. Some men seem to be forced to examine the world view they have accepted and to find out how this view of spiritual reality fits with their understanding. Thinking in this direction, however, cannot be restricted to logical thought if one is to find the meaning of Christianity. This meaning simply eludes the man who does not let his logic spring from symbolic and mythological thought, for it is in this way that one comes to understand the reality of this victory and its power.

It is no easy matter to bring all of one's ideas together in one model of reality. This is hard work, the kind of work that most of us want someone else to do for us. It is helpful to realize, however, that conviction arises more out of personal experience or experiences of others than it does out of logic. In one discussion Jung had to remind me that in Latin the word conviction itself means *to be conquered.* One is seldom conquered by his thought, but more often by his experience.

If one takes the spiritual myth of Christianity as an hypothesis and acts as if it were true, then he will test it as the scientist does his theory. If it is confirmed in his experience—if living and acting and praying as if Christ has conquered brings one a sense of victory and freedom and creative power and leads to positive action—then one is likely to be convinced. If this happens over and over again, then the conviction grows and deepens. At this point, if this conviction is to become the rock on which a whole life is built, one then needs a theology of experience which can be tested out. This is what I have tried to provide in the last half of my book *Encounter with God.*

In studying the great dogmas and doctrines of the church, it is amazing to realize how seldom these dogmas and doctrines were arrived at by logical thought. Rather they were the statements of the experience of those great Christians who shared similar experiences with each other and who sat in the councils of the church, and decided that this was what happened, no matter how paradoxical it seemed. In these dogmas the early Christians were reflecting upon their own lived experiences of the victory which Christ had won for them, and they nearly always expressed it mythologically, in ways that convinced men. Where belief rests upon experience, it usually has this convincing power for others who are seeking to find their way.

Imagination and Quiet

The other main way in which men share in the victory of Christ is by using the imaginative powers of the human soul. Through imagination we are given a powerful method of both opening up experience and finding the symbols and mythological images to express that experience so that it can be thought about and shared with others. Although most moderns have forgotten this use of imagination, it is actually one way we can enter the spiritual world and confront the powers of darkness and light. Conviction about their reality comes when one does experience entering this realm and finds that he is able to influence these forces, and finds that there is a change in both his inner and his outer life, and a change also in the lives of others.

At the same time one finds that he cannot control these powers in himself or others. He can start something happening, but the results are determined by powers greater than most human beings can handle by themselves. One finds that he faces destructive forces which are free to move in and out of the depths of every human soul. This is what the fathers of the church meant by original sin; the forces of evil and destructiveness have a foothold in every one of us. But once the doorway of imagination is found, one finds that they can be confronted if one is actively trying to live in the way that Christ lived His life. Then one is given the power to call imaginatively upon the living Christ, using both inner and outer symbols. This is the only conscious way I know of—by sharing both actively and imaginatively in that life and its magnificent victory—that a man can find freedom from the destructive forces which otherwise keep a free hand by remaining unconscious to him.

It is almost impossible, however, to find this doorway to the unconscious, the realm of spirit, unless one temporarily silences all outer activity. The reality of the meditational way does not open up while we are still holding onto the steering wheel or using the telephone or rushing around with a dustrag in one hand. The first step is to cease physical activity completely for a period of time, sitting quietly in a chair, relaxed and alone. Then one must silence the inner conversation with himself, quietly pushing back the images which keep flowing in from the outside world and from the ego, and keep at it until they subside. Slowly, gently, all thoughts and inner desires are put away into the pending file. This must be done gently, patiently, because a brusque or violent attempt only arouses them to more activity. It is a good deal like eating an artichoke; anyone who tried to take one bite from the top of an artichoke would get nothing but a mouthful of thistles, and the same thing is true in approaching the world of spirit. It takes patience to peel one leaf off at a time.

Without letting go of the outer world, one seldom finds the door to the inner world of spirit. Introversion is an inescapable aspect of the inner journey, a journey that cannot be hurried. If one tries to force meditation, the images cannot flow. Even if he succeeds in pushing out personal desires, he will find himself using concepts rather than images. This is why every devotional master from Jesus to Thomas Merton suggests times of quiet. The practice of silence—which must be tried rather than explained —has been almost universal among those who have found the reality of the spiritual realm through images.

This is the basic meaning of the command to keep holy the Sabbath day. It explains the practices of the Trappists and the Quakers. It crops up in Kierkegaard's delightful quip that you can measure the amount of soul a man has by the amount of silence he needs. He goes on to suggest that the modern age has grown so far from the ideals of a more spiritual age that modern men see no use for silence except as a punishment for incorrigible prisoners. Yet this is not so odd, Kierkegaard reflects, since men of spirit are treated like criminals by the modern world.

Personally I find that I need three kinds of quiet time if I am to keep a healthy meditational life. First of all I need some time daily, perhaps twenty minutes or more. I need this time to reflect back over the day and then to be still and see what emerges out of listening. About once a week I need a longer period of time for a more complete spiritual housecleaning, and at that time I take some dream or phantasy or a Bible story and let these images spin out their meaning for me. At least once a year I need a full day or two in which to get to the bottom of things and see which way the spiritual wind is blowing and which way it would take me.

As one does become still, utterly still and passive, it seems at first as if there were no escape from a black void, an abyss which threatens to swallow the entire person. But surprisingly this does not happen. Slowly, instead of the blackness there is a picture which comes from one side. Images and life begin to move before one's eyes. Inexplicably one is drawn into a whole new world, a world of spirit. I have seldom known anyone who really tried this state of silence who did not find it to be so. Whenever one is truly still and blank from an ego point of view, he does not find himself coming into nothingness, but rather into a limitless world filled with images from some other source. When our ego consciousness has let go of control, the same power which comes to us in dreams during sleep comes to life *consciously,* and we find that the spiritual world is very close and very real to us.

This kind of silence can lead to the discovery that the images and the motifs which arise from within one's self, are operating spontaneously within one's own mind and psyche. Through this naked or free flow of a person's own imagination, he can go on to discover that the myths still live within him, offering a creative connection with the depths of his own life. For example, in imagination one may find the image of the Medusa or the Hercules or the Christ in some new form. It is then even more creative for a person to learn to deal with the mythological images which move at this level of one's being by becoming active himself in the stream of pictures and stories as they form. The person who thus uses his own dreams and his own inner phantasy by following their lead, can come into touch with a whole realm of being from which most people are cut off. Then, the power of Christ's victory over evil and death can open up to him, and as he shares imaginatively in it, his outer life in some way will come to share this victory both psychologically and physically.

If this process can actually offer the results of Christ's victory in our outer lives, it is worth some time and trouble to learn and to use it. Before doing this, one should know one other remarkable fact about inner quiet. Although this inner silence is entered into alone, it is often easier to enter it within a group who are all seeking to be silent. A group of people who are trying to be still together acts almost as a catalyst for one's own silence. And there is a corollary. Although our modern culture has cut us off from these images which flow from some other source than the ego, they are both real and very powerful in our lives, and often very dangerous. It is best not to go this way alone, but with the help and guidance of some wise friend. We need to talk over the images that come with someone who knows this world of spirit and is also versed in other facets of human experience.

It is a fact that the spiritual world is so close that it is possible for any one of us to step over into it as the pictures from it unfold. This is like stepping across to the stage and into the middle of a play that is being enacted. For better or for worse, one can change the action which is going on. And when one changes the action as it unfolds, then he has actually altered the mythological configuration of his life, thus bringing about a change in life's outer events.

This method has been tried by many people who have found it helpful; for many, in fact, it was the only way they could reach their specific, inner problems. Two examples from my own experience will help to show how this can come about. The process is the same for practically everyone I have known who used it. It starts, not with an image from ritual or story, but with one's own inner silence. One simply becomes utterly still, waiting for whatever inner images arise.

Stepping Across the Threshold

When I become silent, sometimes what comes to me is that I see myself on a busy street of a crowded city. I am caught up in crowds of people coming and going without knowing where they are going or why. There is a confusion of sounds, voices of hawkers, loud conversations, traffic noises, and there is no time to be quiet. I rush back and forth with them, and suddenly it is like a Saks-34th Street sale. It is as if there would never be another chance to get into this store building. I am blinded by the bright lights. And just when it seems I can no longer stand this, I realize that I can walk out of there. I go down the street to find myself entering a quiet and shabby little room.

It turns out to be my own, my soul room or spiritual home, and it does not have a very proud appearance. It is a dull and a drab room, not a well-kept sanctuary. Even in this place the television is on full blast; apparently I was afraid to be alone.

Finally in desperation—and how else could I come to myself except in desperation?—I turn off all the intrusive sound and simply lie down and think about the drab sordidness of my oatmeal-papered soul-room. It is then that I realize how frightened I am and how powerless I am. There are several doors to this room. Over one hangs a huge spiderweb in which I see old thoughts, discarded before they were played out, and I watch the spider start to work again. Then a door on the left clatters and bangs, and from it emerge, one by one, the specters of my fears and anxieties, my weaknesses, sins and guilts. Some are represented by the persons I have associated with them, while others come as black and ugly demons to torment me, or they appear as animals. I know the fear of being destroyed now, and I cower. But all at once I recall that I have been saved through the power of Christ. From the depths of despair I force myself to remember that he has defeated these creatures of hell and that he has risen victorious over them. As I realize this I call, and cry out to the Christ, "Come and help me!"

Gently a door on the right side of my soul room opens, and the Christ steps in, with a lantern in his hand, a crown of thorns upon his head, the marks of the nails visible upon his hands and his sandaled feet. A great ruby fastens his gold cloak around his shoulders. At that moment the demons tremble and begin to flee. As the specters of my sins and guilts vanish, I am left alone with the Lord of heaven and hell. I kneel before him, and he raises me to my feet, embracing me with the affection of a father for a child, and we sit and talk. He does not say that there is nothing to fear, but he says, "Lo, I am with you always, even to the end of the world." Later, when we sit at the table, he provides bread and wine, heavenly food, and I am sustained. And I hear him say, "Behold, I stand at the door and knock; if any man will hear my voice and open the door, I will come in to him, and will sup with him, and he with me."

Returning from this state of silence, of active listening, one actually finds that the heaviness and anxiety of his soul begin to lift. Stepping into the center of the soul and then bringing the Christ into it, the one who has risen victorious, actually changes the condition of a man's soul. It works. In this way one is allowing the creative and positive spiritual reality of the risen Christ to enter and act effectively in his life. It is not just a matter of ideas, but of spiritual reality with which one deals in the meditative state.

In contrast let us look for a moment at another way of dealing with the depth of human experience. Virginia Woolf, the brilliant, experimental novelist of the twenties and thirties, was one who was forced to go into the very depth of herself, analyzing every image of her own soul, coming into direct confrontation with the unconscious. But she believed she was liberated, that she was free. She had no need for Christian mythology or images. And what happened to Virginia Woolf? After each of her books she was so exhausted that she had long periods of depression, and finally of physical illness. When her last work, *Between the Acts,* was completed, Virginia Woolf went to the river which flowed near her home and threw herself in and was drowned.

On the surface one can account for this tragedy solely in terms of this gifted woman's outer experiences. But in reality we human beings are all in much the same strange position. We have all suffered traumas which could be bandaged over. Yet if we don't deal with the depths, we either live superficial lives, or else we are tormented by neurosis, or psychosomatic illness, or fits of depression or anger. And if we do deal with them, we run the danger of being swamped by what we find.

There is only one way that I know of to live at all safely with deep human experience and avoid just skimming the surface, and that is to bring the power of the risen, victorious Christ imaginatively into our lives, keeping him as a constant companion in real living. Otherwise we may go the same way as Virginia Woolf, or Herman Melville who went mad after writing Moby Dick, or Nietzsche who never recovered sanity after going into the depth of his images. It doesn't seem fair that we must choose between superficiality or danger. It is possible to make the choice with confidence only because there *is* a power greater than ourselves standing by ready to help us.

Dealing with spiritual reality is never a joy ride, never. Although the word *never* must be used sparingly, it applies here. When one faces the immense and very real domain of spirit, he finds not only those unpleasant things about himself of which he had been unconscious, half by choice, but also the reality of naked evil. In addition he must deal with archetypal forces which work upon the psyche sometimes for good and sometimes for evil. There is no way of spiritual growth and development that I know of which does not involve tension, frustration, pain and suffering. One need not seek pain and suffering. Enough will come of its own. The Christ is there to release us from this suffering, but he can release us only from as much as we are willing to bear. Substituting physical illness for inner psychic pain, however, does not have the same creative effect, and in most people it leads only to sterility and bitterness.

The way of spirit is a difficult way, a way for the courageous, the way of the cross in the deepest and finest sense. Jesus knew what he was talking about when he said that his followers would have to pick up their crosses to follow him. In fact, I know of only one good reason for entering into this realm where there is such difficulty and tension. In the end, *not* doing it is usually many times more painful and less creative. My own following of this way does not spring from any great nobility; rather I find that the way of honest confrontation is less painful and destructive than avoiding it. And at the end of the road the Christ waits to welcome and greet me, and make it worthwhile. At the same time, when I am confronting the dark and ugly things within me, both the personal and the metaphysical ones, I am much less likely to inflict them on other people around me. Let us now look at another example of how this inner difficulty can be handled.

There are times in the silence when I see myself hurrying along a great, level highway, with a crowd of people hustling each other along for no reason at all. Suddenly I see myself stop, stand stock-still, and ask the travelers rushing by: Is there any meaning to all this rush? Doesn't this road lead from nowhere to nowhere? They say that I am mad to stop, and when I look around, I see that they are right. I will be left alone in a desert without food or water. But still, something inside of me tells me that I must turn aside, and I sit down by the road and watch them jostle and race each other out of sight.

When it is quiet, I look around and for the first time see a faint path leading off to the left towards a forbidding mountain pass. Fearfully, I set out and soon find myself in a canyon. There a spring of living water wells out of the rock and flows into a tiny orchard, where it disappears into the ground. In this oasis there are other travelers who had lost their bearings on the great highway and turned aside. We find sustenance enough for the moment, and courage to start out once more on the rough path, this time together. We follow it through the mountains and down into a valley, watered and green, which seems to be the place that is meant for us, a heavenly Jerusalem. There the King and the Christ are waiting to bring us fresh garments and a feast, to show us the rooms which had long since been prepared for us.

As I began to carry this kind of creative and active imagination into my day to day life, trying to offer some of the same reality to others, I began to find that it is possible to call upon the Christ at any time. One can find Him whenever reality becomes threatening and dangerous. He is there. This is the meaning of Christian meditation, and the images with which one can start are limitless. They can originate in spontaneous phantasy, or they may be taken from dreams with all of their strange symbolism. Once I took the dream-image of a turtle and followed its lead wherever it wished to go. In my dream it had come up out of the sea and spoken to me, and I followed it in free imagination to a new land where I learned enough about myself to assure you that if a dream animal should ever try to speak to you, it would be most wise to listen with your imagination.

One friend of mine, at a time when he was in serious difficulty, saw himself aboard a floundering ship on a raging sea; he called in terror to the Christ and saw him come and pilot the ship, with all aboard, into a safe port. This friend learned the power of the image from his experience, for he found a fresh burst of energy and a new outlook on his own problems. I have known of other experiences in which the person was lost in a deep cave or in a foreign city and was led to find a treasure of great value.

The important thing is to let the images flow from the depths of one's self, realizing that there is nothing to fear if one is able to call upon the living Christ who can handle any situation in a man's life. How else can a man discover the mysterious and hidden depths of himself except by allowing his phantasy to lead him? Certainly he cannot find victorious power over these hidden forces unless he finds some way to become conscious of them, to encounter them so that they do not go on working unconsciously in the psyche. Obviously it is difficult to conquer what one does not face.

To take the first step towards an encounter with these spiritual forces one must turn aside from logical and rational consideration of life and allow the images, the mythological patterns to arise in him. This is both something we do and something which simply happens to us. It is probably most effective when the phantasy is recorded, for some people in writing or talking into a tape recorder, for others by painting the images or modeling them in clay. The images and motifs then become more concrete and thus are easier to look at objectively. They are also easier to enter into again. But in doing so, it is very necessary for most people to have the help and guidance of another person who has gone this way before and is trained to understand the human psyche in its relation to the spiritual world. There is reason to repeat that *this is a dangerous way to go alone.* As a man allows this kind of phantasy to move within him, he finds that the great mythological motifs, springing from within himself, still act with powerful and dynamic effect on human life.

He finds that he is able, through his own will, to enter into communication with this reality and actually influence it. But this does not happen through logical or rational thought, but through the power of imagination. By means of active imagination a man can discover this spiritual world, which is not subject to the action of reason or logic, and through imagination he can take part in its real and powerful influence upon his own life. This startling thought, which is today the discovery of a few medical scientists and their patients, was once known to many people, for it was once the contention and practice of historical Christianity.

As medical men have realized, four sets of emotions

plague modern man and destroy him both physically and emotionally. One of them is the fear-anxiety-apprehension syndrome, which leaves one fearful that there is no help for man. He stands against a meaningless universe which is amoral, ambivalent, and cares nothing for man, if it is not actually hostile to him. How can a man ever be free of the destructiveness of this emotion unless he believes that there is some power in the universe which cares for him? But as the fear is expressed in images, and the caring Christ is brought to help face them, this fear and its allies must either turn and show another face, or be put to flight. And I know personally of no other way of doing it.

Then there is the emotion of anger-hostility-hatred, which does have value when it is kept from becoming dominant. It provides the essential energy to go out and tackle the world, just as fear offers the needed caution that some people lack. When the hatred syndrome gets into full swing, it is usually because the person is afraid. Most often hostility is the direct reaction to powerlessness; it is the coverup for fear. Again, how can a man handle the deep anger within him unless there is some reality which cares enough to give meaning? In a universe which lacks this, what alternatives are there but the continual retreat of fear, or the repeated explosions of hatred against anyone who becomes an obstacle, including even one's self. And again, I know of no healing for hostility except the experience of the loving Christ who cared enough to die, and to return resurrected to keep showing men this healing.

The emotion of depression and guilt, of psychic pain and abiding sorrow can be touched only as one finds his life imaginatively cared for, forgiven, restored. Who else can bring this healing but the Christ figure? And finally there is the emotion of destructive egotism, which may well be another form of fear. What hell it creates, destroying marriages, building walls between people, those fortresses that are required by fear. Yet how can any of us escape egotism unless he knows in reality and in imagination a power greater than himself which wishes to guide him through the treacherous passages that are found in every life? Only the Christ offers to accept man as he is, and bring him restoration and wholeness.

I know of no way to handle these emotions, medically or any other way, except to allow them to emerge in images, and then to be touched by the reality of the victorious Christ, both imaginatively and through the Holy Spirit. If it is true that this healing is available, there is probably nothing more important for this world of ours than for us to know and experience the living myth of Christianity. How can we approach its reality once more?

Allowing the Biblical Myth To Live

When one is able to follow the flow of images and phantasy in the way we have described, sooner or later he finds that he can enter another dimension of reality, and that here he can tap the source of most of the myths of mankind. He finds that the psyche today still weaves the same kind of living stories to which men have related their lives through religious ritual all through the centuries. One can also allow the same imaginative process to play upon some story from religious literature, and let it become a part of the imagination and so of life. By entering this process fully, one becomes a part of the myth himself. As it comes alive within him, he shares in its power and so is connected with the depths of the unconscious, with spiritual reality. Probably the best way of explaining this is to illustrate it; let me give you three examples from the Biblical narrative, each of which suggests the way of reviving the myth of Christianity so that it may work in our lives again.

At Christmas time one may take the story of Mary

coming with Joseph to bear the Christ child in Bethlehem.
By identifying with Mary, one travels the long road from
Nazareth to Bethlehem with her. It is not an easy way,
when one must travel on donkey over the rocky arroyos
and ridges of the desert. Gradually a picture comes into
focus; there is a quiet rest watching the play of water in
a tiny stream, and then the dust and heat of the sun. It
is no easy task to bear the Christ child within one's self.
The journey towards the birth is fraught with difficulties
and dangers, perhaps a marauding band, or the cutting
wind. One is even rebuffed at the inn where the birth
might have been comfortable. And so the child is born in
the stable, in the least acceptable place of one's life, not
at all the place that would be hoped for.

Yet the child is born and there is joy. And one says,
I have come this far; I will go on with Mary. Almost
immediately there are forces which seek to destroy the
child, the new life in one, and he must flee to a foreign
land and stay there until these ruling forces are dead.
Again pictures come, of the strange sights and sounds in
the land of exile, of trying to find someone who speaks
the same language, anyone who can understand. When at
last one does return to his native land, he must go a cir-
cuitous route to find a place of haven, but in this haven
there is no person who knows the hardships or the fears,
or the reason for them. . . . In this way one can allow the
phantasy to wander where it will, using the story as a base
and letting the imagination play creatively to offer new
images and new insights.

If ever there was a saga of the way of the soul, the
way towards new life and transformation within one's self,
this meditation on the story of Mary can provide it. As we
see and feel the difficulties, the joy which Mary had in
physically bringing forth the Christ child, then we are not
so dismayed at the task of bringing the spiritual birth to
place within ourselves. This is the imaginative preparation

which makes the new life within us a possibility. FOR THAT WHICH WE HAVE NEVER IMAGINED AS POSSIBLE SPIRITUALLY WITHIN OURSELVES CAN SELDOM TAKE PLACE IN US. Mythology and meditation upon it help to prepare the way for spiritual growth within the individual.

Another story which is known to all of us is the one of the good Samaritan. Most people take this story as a parable which tells us to be good to people in trouble, but let us see what mythological meaning it holds. If it is our soul who is the traveler from Jerusalem to Jericho, then what is it within *us* that hides in the rocks to ambush and rob and leave us half dead by the side of the road? Were we careful enough in setting out upon the perilous route from Jerusalem to Jericho? What forces in our lives hold up their robes and get by the injured part of us, like the priest and the Levite, with as little notice as possible? In other words, what are the traditional parts of us which will give us no help in restoring the wounded, broken parts of our psyches? How little help we can expect from these conventional sides of ourselves who go along keeping their skirts respectably clean.

And the Samaritan? Undoubtedly the injured man lying by the road would have avoided sitting down or even speaking with a Samaritan under ordinary circumstances. Who is he but the one who is rejected and despised, that part of our darkness, our hidden side with which we will have nothing to do so long as things seem to be going well. Yet how often the healing of our brokenness comes only from this rejected part of ourselves, from some part of the unconscious from which we have been separated.... Again, how magnificently this parable tells of the mythological journey of the soul. Should we be surprised to find such depth of meaning in Jesus of Nazareth if He is the one who Christians have maintained that He is?

Again, let us take the story of Lazarus, once again

approaching what the myth itself can mean to us, rather than trying to decide sight unseen, as most people do, whether to believe or just to shrug off the actual event of the raising from the dead. Again we must remind ourselves that myth and history are not mutually exclusive categories. I happen to believe that the event actually occurred as it is related in the Bible, and at the same time I believe that it is very fruitful for us to appreciate its mythological meaning as well.

Some part of each of us, like Lazarus, has died. Perhaps it should have died. Perhaps there can be no really new life until parts of us do die and are buried. This may have been the reason that Jesus waited for two days after he had been told of his friend's illness. At any rate when he reached the place, he found that Lazarus had already been buried, and he showed the depth of feeling that he had for this friend who had died. Jesus wept. Unless there is genuine feeling, sorrow, inner weeping, there can be no rebirth out of death; the pain and the tears are needed to bring back to life that part of ourselves which we have lost. This rebirth is not an intellectual process, like a decision to turn in the spare tire on a retread. It is as painful and as wonderful as any childbirth.

We are told then that Jesus sighed again, and went to the tomb to command that the stone be taken away. Unless there is action, there can be no rebirth. Sitting apart and wishing it will not accomplish the new life; someone must move the stone so that there is a possibility of coming forth. But there was also one who complained that there would be a bad smell, since Lazarus had been in the tomb for four days; and Jesus told them to have faith, and they moved the stone. How can there ever be rebirth when we refuse to face the stench of our mistakes, our sins, our faults, and our inner evils and turmoil? Those who want a nice, surgical resurrection, who want to find a way of listerine purity, are going to wait forever, for no stench no resurrection! With a loud voice Jesus commanded Lazarus to come forth after praying to God for help. Again there must be feeling, a direct and definite desire that the dead part of us be raised from the dead, expressed by a prayer for resurrection, a fervent one, and a loud cry for it, before the Lazarus in us can come forth. When he did come out, still bound, Jesus told the people to unbind him and set him free. How often do people find a taste of new life or new spirit and then discover that it is just too dangerous to face this re-born part of themselves. This is the final, essential command; the new life must be set free if it is not to be smothered and die again. . . . Here again is a mythological motif marvelously portrayed in the Biblical story.

It was from a meditation much like this that one young man found himself after we had spent many months in a counseling relationship without being able to pierce to the core of his problem. He had come to me tied up in knots psychologically; he was at a dead end in life, inhibited and unable to reach out of himself. He could see himself only in the mirror of a friend he would admire for a few weeks or a teacher whose life he would decide he must follow. But there was never energy enough released to go ahead and change, and he could not find any reason for the constriction which bound him.

One Sunday he heard a sermon which presented the story of Lazarus from this mythological point of view. Two nights later the young man had a dream in which he saw himself standing with his girl friend beside a casket in which his own brother was about to be buried. In the dream he was able, with the girl's help, to raise his brother from death. As he worked with this dream and began to understand it, he felt that it was directing him to an important idea. He saw that he had to let a part of himself—the part his brother represented—be raised from death as Lazarus was, and that he really needed the help of his girl friend in the task. As a result he was freed to marry the girl, and to become free himself from the inhibitions which had crippled his life until then.

This kind of imaginative or mythological reading of the scriptures of any religion can provide insights and directions for the living of life which have a value beyond description. It can do this because it establishes a connection with the depth of the unconscious within one's self, and so with the spiritual world. The reason so few people appreciate the Bible and our vast store of other mythological literature is because they try to understand it only intellectually, and they then fail to let it establish any such connection with themselves and the reality of the spiritual world. This is the work of true meditation.

Once one has solved an intellectual problem, then one can use the results of the solution without going back over the process step by step. It is different in the mythical encounter, which gives a different purpose to the meditational way. What has been accomplished once must still be done again and again. To return to our image of the mechanic and the farmer: once the machine is made, it is finished. A little oiling and maintenance is all that is required. The farmer, on the other hand, must return each year to harrow and plough his fields, to add fertilizer to them, to water them where there is no rain and to constantly weed them. Like the farmer, one returns again and again to meditation, with fresh purpose and insight. Meditation is the tilling of the soil of one's soul.

X
Myth
and Sacrament

There is no place where the deepest realities of life can speak to man better than in ritual, in its natural and creative joining of meditation with sacramental action. Once one has found a relation to mythical or spiritual reality, he finds that sharing in religious ritual touches something beyond the human. There are peoples, in far corners of the world, who have not been affected by the exclusively logical and rational attitudes of Western civilization, and for them the rituals of some religious group are the natural collective way of finding relationship with spiritual reality. But this does not always mean a purpose like the Christian one. The powers of that realm can also be tapped for questionable ends, like the aim of a war dance to put the warrior in touch with the tribal equivalent of Mars, and send him out with new power to strike the enemy with fury.

Modern man has his mythological side too, with more action than consciousness in it. In his rituals for war the power of the unconscious and the demonic have broken through with compelling force. When people feel bored and short on meaning, they can go to war and be empowered again. And Western man in his enthusiasm for two world wars in our own time has shown that he can be as unconscious as the most primitive bushman.

Of course, the modern world also has rituals of reconciliation, healing and transformation, but these are more demanding. Unfortunately it appears that when the unconscious or spiritual realm is left on its own without conscious effort, only its destructive side breaks through. Reconciliation and transformation do not often take place without conscious preparation. And part of the preparation is to become conscious of the realities which make ritual and sacrament truly meaningful, truly carriers of the power of Christ. This is one of the great values of meditation; as we begin to think and act mythologically, meditation helps us throw open the sacramental door to the realities which transmit inner and spiritual grace.

Ritual actions speak to the total man, to the very depth of him. When man brings only his logical mind with its materialistic conviction to his rituals, he walls off the rest of his being from their transforming power. We live in a world that has largely forgotten the way sacraments speak to men. Instead, it looks to Santa Claus and the Easter egg, with their outright, one-sided materialism, for meaning our two greatest religious festivals. It is no wonder that among modern men, even regular church-goers, there are so few who bring more than a part of themselves to the sacraments, even though our world needs so much to be open to their full influence. Of course just being there makes some difference, but not the difference it could make.

The Christian sacraments are the most highly developed and most profound rituals man has ever had. When man turns away from these rituals, then he generally picks far less creative, less total ones, like a ritual of mating, or one of war. Man is going to be religious about something, because that seems to be his nature. A few years ago I found a cartoon which expressed this so well that I cut it out and had it framed. It shows two parents finding their children involved in a weird voodoo ritual, complete with altar, idols and pins. One parent is blithely saying: "See, I told you they'd find their own religion if we just let them alone!" We ignore religion at our peril, because almost invariably the demonic elements find a way to take over.

The problem, however, is not how to impose religious ideas on gentle and sensitive minds, but rather how to let them see the heights of which ritual action is capable. Nor is there a choice between myth or no myth. Instead the choice is between myth which has been forged out of a creative struggle, out of the agony of both man and God, and myth which is juvenile or even barbaric. As we have suggested, the noble savage—the nobility of simple, un-conscious man—is pure illusion. One finds that, either he has quite a high-grade religion, or more often he is ruled like the boys in Golding's *Lord of the Flies,* or the Nazis described by Elie Wiesel with such fearful reality in *Night,* his memoir of the death camps.

It was Jung who noted that the Christian dogmatic structure offered the finest system of psychotherapy man had ever had. But many men have become cut off from these Christian formulations and rituals, and often they are not satisfied with the surface of life, or are unable to stay afloat. Then one is forced into a naked confrontation within, which can be made successfully only by a few especially gifted people. Those who have penetrated the deepest tell of much the same reality as that described by the best of Christianity. Some men apparently have to make this confrontation for themselves. But for most of us the church needs to provide a rich and varied way through its sacramental and meditational life. As Jung and certain of his followers have tried to show, a vital Chris-tianity can provide the way for men to continue the heal-ing of psychotherapy and go on beyond it.

The two most vital rituals of the church are the com-munion or Mass (the Eucharist), and baptism. We can do no greater disservice to modern man than to try to ration-

ritual actions are outmoded, but that modern man is
alize these services. The trouble is not that sacramental,
primitive religiously. He has gone overboard on one side,
and is tilting the boat. He needs the services of the church,
its rituals, to pull him back to life and meaning. He needs
those that are intimate and informal, and also the numinous sacraments which arouse the mythical and archetypal
depths within him. Let us look at the meaning these
sacraments offer.

The Symbols of Transformation

In the communion service one steps into the mythological setting of the hero preparing for the sacrifice.
Candles are lit, invoking not just the present-day image
of "light," but the ancient symbol of bringing light into
the blackness of night as in the time of Christ. The priest
may wear vestments that represent the clothes Christ
wore, and the altar is set with vessels representing the very
cup and plate he used. Bread and wine are brought
forward, both of them symbols from the time of Christ.
The bread speaks of the Great Mother, the all-nourishing,
the earthy which can also turn and destroy, and this is the
element offered first. The wine is a symbol of gaiety,
abandonment, and freedom, of daring and also dangerous
masculinity.

First these elements are used in the ritual enactment
of the last supper of Christ with his disciples. Then the
bread is broken, symbolizing the death of Christ on the
cross, and finally the people come forward to share in his
new life. Those who receive the sacrament are participating in the symbolic meaning of the great mother and the
god of wine, and the transformation and union of these
realities in the Christ; they share in the sacrifice he had
to make to bring this union, and in his death and resurrec-

tion. The very action has meaning even if they do not understand it—so long as the myth is not, either consciously or unconsciously, despised and downgraded.

Often people who participate in the service are renewed without any knowledge of why it has happened. Myth and ritual do not have to be understood to be effective. Indeed too much attempt to understand consciously and rationally may rob them of their very effectiveness. As we have tried to suggest, myth represents an actual pattern available to be lived; by taking part in its ritual, the participant experiences the myth, lives it and makes it a part of himself. One reason for the strength of Roman Catholicism is that the Mass is a living reality to many of its people. Because the power of the myth is alive in it, the Mass brings its participants into creative contact with the realities of the spiritual world, with the unconscious.

One of Dr. Jung's most profound writings is his paper on "Transformation Symbolism in the Mass."[1] Here he points out the ways in which this service offers transformation and renewal, showing why it is one of the most meaningful of all rituals. He shows that throughout history men have tried to come to this idea of sacrifice and renewal, sometimes expressing it in the crudest ways. Then, with the Christian understanding of Christ as the incarnation of God—the transforming center of reality—the idea of creative contact with that center through the Mass became possible. In it those deepest efforts of men to reach for this idea are brought to fruition, to their highest expression.

Those who think that the Catholic Church is losing its young people because the symbols of the Mass are out of date simply do not know the dream life of the average college student. Students brought up in parochial school or within the religious tradition often talk that way today. But how often the very ones who say they have outgrown the symbols and meanings of Christianity come to me to talk over dreams they have had in which we find the same images recurring with numinous power. They are not dead. When a student says they no longer have meaning for him, he is usually reacting to authoritarian indoctrination, not to the myth and practices of Christianity.

Other sacraments of the church have just as much mythological meaning. Have you ever thought about the real meaning of your own baptism? This is not easy for Protestants; a gentle sprinkling is about all that is left of the violent significance of the act in the primitive church. Those early candidates for the saving power of Christ were often lowered into a cistern or a well and actually immersed three times. As one went under the water, he was dying with Christ, and as he rose up out of it, he was rising to new life. Although hardly anyone has this experience today, its symbolic meaning is still alive for those who are sensitive to the reality of the myth.

A few months ago a woman who had been immersed as an adult made a point of describing to me her own experience of baptism and its meaningfulness. She said that as she was lying under the water trusting only the strong arms of the one who was baptizing her, it was indeed a giving up of herself. As she came up out of the water, it was to a new life in reality. In telling me she realized for the first time the full meaning of her experience, the symbolic meaning of stripping oneself, ready to accept new life. The early Christian converts were usually baptized on Easter Even, the day before Easter, symbolizing the fact that they had died with Christ and would rise again with him.

As we shall see, in connection with another rite, there are various other ways in which this transformation is still suggested in the Roman rituals. In addition, students like the church historian Fr. Hugo Rahner show how deeply the ritual washing and other symbols of baptism go in human history.[2] The ancient idea that there are eight facets to the whole personality, which also seems to be a reality, is represented by the octagonal baptistries and the eight-sided fonts commonly used. Other symbols, from the fire of the baptismal candle extinguished in the water to the form of blessing it, and even the sign of the cross made on the person's head, can be traced in religious rituals everywhere. Again, Christian baptism springs from the deepest yearnings of man to find his real meaning, and it draws them together into the highest form man has known. Charles Williams' novel *All Hallow's Eve* is an attempt to portray this reality in fictional form. Understood as a real experience of death and resurrection, of new life, what is more important for men than this rite of baptism, and where could it have any more meaning than within the Christian mythological framework?

In the sacrament of laying on of hands for healing we find a more exclusively Christian meaning. This service, by repeating the apostolic act, expresses the mythological understanding of the reality of healing, (which I have shown in some detail in my recent book *Healing and Christianity*). As the person who needs healing kneels to be touched by the priest, it is as if the apostles laid their hands upon him, asking release and renewal. Priests of the Greek Orthodox church often repeat this rite for a sick person on seven successive days, if possible with seven priests taking part. Here is a sacramental enhancing of the mystery of the human touch. So much of concern and love can be conveyed by the touch, and in the sacrament of laying on of hands the touch of man becomes the touch of the Christ, bringing healing power and concern, the very essence of His mission to man.

Sacramental anointing with oil for healing is also frequently used in the Greek church. The sacramental use of oil is probably far older than history, and oil is still used for the anointing of kings in England. It is that by which the spirit is conferred. Oil is a symbol of the good things of life, the fatness of the land, the "oil of joy and gladness." Together with wheat and wine it makes the staple of life in the Near East to this day. Symbolically the act of anointing with oil stands for the bestowal of greater life and spirit.

Although many priests look askance at the idea of exorcism, and it sometimes takes some doing to find one who will perform an exorcism, this ritual also strikes deeply and powerfully into the human psyche. The fact that a story based on the Catholic understanding of the rite made the best seller lists for so long certainly shows that the idea of evil, and deliverance from it, is not dead.

Exorcism expresses a very ancient mythical understanding that evil spirits which trouble man—or, to use more sophisticated modern language, autonomous complexes—can be cast out of him. The priest who performs an exorcism usually wears purple vestments, signifying penitence. He places his stole around the neck of the person who is possessed, and the person is then sprinkled with holy water, and hands are laid upon him. The priest speaks in a firm and authoritative voice, commanding the spirit to leave. All through the ritual, a crucifix, the effective symbol against evil, is kept in plain sight.

Although we seldom credit his infernal majesty with much sense, he sometimes seems to be wiser than the children of light. There are some very interesting studies of demon possession in the past,[3] and in my own ministry I have certainly been open to the possibility; yet I have seen very few instances of what might be termed the classical pattern of possession. It is my intuition that Satan does not use this particular manifestation of power today because evil spirits are so little believed in by our society. Instead, possession today takes the form of neurosis or psychosomatic disease, which often responds well to a kind of exorcism.

This ancient rite, or vestiges of it, also goes hand in hand with other sacraments of the Roman Catholic Church. Before a person can be baptized and brought into the body of Christ, he must be cleansed. Salt is blessed and placed in the mouth of the candidate, and one end of the priest's stole is placed over his shoulder. If an adult is being baptized, the priest blows three times into his face, signifying the expulsion of the devil. The sign of the cross is used on several parts of the candidate's body, sometimes being made in saliva. The oil of chrism, with which a baptized person is anointed, is known as the "oil of exorcism," because, like other objects which are to be dedicated to God, the devil is cast out before it is blessed.

In receiving confirmation the person is anointed with this same oil and then is struck lightly on the cheek, reminding him that suffering may be involved in the life he is entering. This is but a sampling of the symbolic and mythological richness of historic Christianity, whose ritual actions continue to speak with ever fresh significance of the healing and transformation and growth which Christ brings to men. These actions can be amplified over and over without exhausting their meanings.

I wonder how many of us have had experiences like these, with their deep imprint on one's religious life. What are the days you recall as a child in the church? Aren't they the days when you did something outward which was symbolic of an inward fact? For some of us there may be the palms from far off which decked the church on a blustery Palm Sunday, and the blessing of the palm crosses we carried home. We may remember how these were gathered up and burned the next year on Ash Wednesday to make the strange cross of ashes on people's foreheads. Of course we remember Christmas candies or ornaments, and Easter lilies. Easter flowers have become a symbol because we have so few others left; there is a gap in our lives which we try to fill, perhaps by setting up the Christmas crèche once a year. Unless we have an adequate myth, we live starved lives and try to fill them with cheap and inadequate symbols which do not meet our deep need.

How much we human beings need to touch again the deep roots of life through adequate rituals which express great myths and their union with Christian history and with the lives of Christians.

A Final Word

The world of spirit is real. There are forces for good and forces for evil in it, and both the good and evil ones influence our outer material lives, and even the course of history itself. The person who learns to think mythologically and to meditate imaginatively can enter that world. He can also gain entrance to it by participating fully in religious rituals as actions expressing the mythological view of reality. In these ways one is brought into touch with a whole realm of being from which most modern men are almost completely cut off.

When one does enter this realm, he can come under his own steam and take his chances against forces which are more than most men can handle. Or, he can look to the victory won by Jesus of Nazareth on Easter, and share in that victory over evil and darkness, both in this world and the next. The Christ, when he comes to a man, routs the forces of evil which would overwhelm us and brings good where there was evil, peace where there was conflict, love where there was hate, humility where there was pride, compassion where there was envy, and victory where defeat was impending. When Christ comes, he gives the Holy Spirit and its gifts and fruits and powers. And this happens, just as the saints throughout the ages have testified, whenever men make it their serious business to follow Christ in this way.

The real job of religion is to help the individual find his way in this spiritual realm, to help him find the mythological patterns of life and his own destiny in relation to them. Vital religion through its myths helps men come into contact with the realities represented by the images of myth, and such religion then enables them to deal creatively and victoriously with these realities. In so doing, the individual comes to wholeness himself and becomes a creative and effective member of the group.

There is value in the myths of most religions, and men need a variety of approaches to this realm. We are not really wise enough to choose for others on whom life may make different demands. But for modern men of the Western world, the Christian approach is available; it is alive deep within the psyches of most, if not all, of us. And in the end, once men have begun to grow to maturity and are forced to face life consciously, I know of no other approach that can fill their need. There is really no point in putting off the realization that what happened in Judea two thousand years ago has involved us in a myth which is very much alive today, and which we will have to come to in the end anyway.

Christianity offers the most adequate mythological formulation available to men, the most valid description of the inner world which has ever been given. It is a mythological statement which is true to reality. Christianity stands in relation to spiritual reality as the modern atomic theory does to physical reality. It describes spiritual reality as it is and gives us a way of dealing with this reality creatively and confidently. The atomic theory not only describes reality, but through the description gives into our hands the power of the atom for use. Christianity provides the same power over spiritual reality when we take its way of dealing with these realities seriously in thought and action and imaginative meditation.

The person who is cut off from the myth-making function of his own psyche lives only a fragment of the life he could live. What is worse, the man who is purely rational, and so is out of contact with the reality which springs forth spontaneously in dreams and myth, is completely subject to the whims of the negative side of spiritual reality. He has no control over his own spiritual destiny and so is cut off from the meaning and power which are available to human beings.

Life without myth is likely to be dead and sterile, while religion without myth is a flat, rational substitute for the real thing. It has little effect upon life. Without myth, Christianity degenerates either into doctrinal system or into ethical culture. It becomes religionless religion, without much practical value. And men, left without myth, become like puppets, strung up only to the tyranny of the unknown.

Myth and the rituals that spring from it provide the meeting ground in which the nonphysical half of reality makes contact with men. Through myth and ritual man is given help so that he can find his way out to sea and back, over wild and deep waters. And this is as true today, if not more true than in the days when men expected to see giants and heroes and even the divine spark in flesh and blood. It is high time for the church to acknowledge its fascinating mythological territory and start learning how it can help men chart their way through this realm in which God can be found, and yet so many have floundered.

Notes

CHAPTER I

1. This whole question, as it relates to the many and varied religious reactions and movements today, is discussed in some depth by *Time* Magazine in a recent special series called "Second Thoughts About Man." See *Time,* April 9, 1973, pp. 90 ff.
2. The statistics on church attendance and attitudes are discussed in my book *Encounter with God,* Minneapolis, Bethany Fellowship, Inc., 1972, pp. 21 ff.; except for small shifts in total church membership, the *1973 Yearbook of American and Canadian Churches* shows no real change.

   One of the best studies of the present crisis of faith is presented by Andrew M. Greeley in *Priests in the United States: Reflections on a Survey,* Garden City, New York, Doubleday & Company, Inc., 1972.
3. Oppenheimer's remarks were delivered in an address before the annual meeting of the American Psychological Association in 1955. See "Analogy in Science," *The American Psychologist,* Vol. 11, 1956, pp. 134 f.

CHAPTER II

1. Jim Bishop, *The Day Lincoln Was Shot,* Harper & Row, 1955, pp. 54 ff.
2. Lloyd Lewis, *Myths after Lincoln,* New York, Grosset & Dunlap, 1957, p. 290.
3. Lewis, *op. cit.,* pp. 292 f.
4. For two fascinating accounts of John Kennedy's background, from different points of view, see Gail Cameron, *Rose: A Biography of Rose Fitzgerald Kennedy,* New York, G. P. Putnam's Sons, 1971, and the somewhat more judgmental study by Nancy Gager Clinch, *The Kennedy Neurosis: A Psychological Portrait of an American Dynasty,* New York, Grosset & Dunlap, 1973.
5. *Saturday Review,* December 7, 1963, p. 64.

6. A Lincoln-Kennedy penny was minted, but for some reason was not released. It is just now being offered through a mail-order speciality firm.
7. Jess Stearn, *The Miracle Workers: America's Psychic Consultants,* New York, Bantam Books, 1972, p. 150.

CHAPTER III

1. The Old Testament understanding of evil is made quite clear by Rivkah Schärf Kluger in *Satan in the Old Testament,* Evanston, Illinois, Northwestern University Press, 1967.
2. In this book, *The Way of All the Earth: Experiments in Truth and Religion,* New York, The Macmillan Company, 1972, John Dunne helps us to see that the need for religion is universal, and not just a peculiarity of a few people called Christians.
3. Science has begun to see that materialism is based more on faith than on fact. The scientist "knows" something because he has made a good guess, and then has learned by experience that it works given the particular circumstances. But when it comes to discovering universal truth, he simply has to guess again, because we have no way of testing something out under every conceivable circumstance.
4. See Marie-Louise von Franz, *The Feminine in Fairytales,* New York, Spring Publications, 1972.
5. Alexander Heidel, *The Gilgamesh Epic and Old Testament Parallels,* Chicago, The University of Chicago Press, 1963, p. 87.
6. A letter from the Bishop of Winchester to St. Boniface about 723 shows the beginnings of this idea; quoted by H. R. Ellis Davidson, *Gods and Myths of Northern Europe,* Baltimore, Maryland, Penguin Books, 1964, p. 190.
7. C. G. Jung, *Collected Works,* Vol. 10, *(Civilization in Transition),* New York, Pantheon Books, 1964, pp. 184 f.
8. Article on the "Gabar" in the *Encyclopaedia Britannica,* 1968, Vol. 9, p. 1064.
9. The tradename "Mazda Lamps" is still used for the European market.

CHAPTER IV

1. Ezekiel 8:14.
2. J. K. S. Reid, *Our Life in Christ,* Aberdeen, Scotland, S.C.M. Press, 1963, p. 64.

CHAPTER V

1. In *The Quest of the Historical Jesus,* (London, Adam and Charles Black, 1948), Albert Schweitzer shows in detail the kind of things that were studied by these nineteenth century scholars. This work was first published in 1906.
2. One book based on this kind of thinking is *The Passover Plot* by Hugh J. Schonfield, in which he constructs an elaborate—almost "Mission-Impossible"—story to explain the resurrection as a pre-arranged plot between Jesus and a secret group of followers who used drugs to keep him from actually dying on the cross; (New York, Bantam Books, Inc., 1967).

CHAPTER VI

1. Sir James George Frazer and the twelve weighty volumes of *The Golden Bough* are still cited everywhere as if these nineteenth century ideas were the last word on understanding mythology. The fact that Frazer went to so much trouble to discredit the religious use of myth really should alert some of us to ask why, if he was merely tilting with windmills, with an unreality, was it worth all that effort? Or is there a reality which Frazer felt he needed to dominate by the use of his rational powers?
2. Johan Huizinga has written wisely and deeply on the importance of play to human life, in his book *Homo Ludens: A Study of the Play Element in Culture,* Boston, Beacon Press, 1955.
3. E. R. Dodds gives ample evidence of the Greek appreciation for mythical thinking and experience in his masterful study, *The Greeks and the Irrational,* Boston, Beacon Press, 1957. Dodds is Regius Professor of Greek at Oxford University.
4. For further understanding of the relation between emotions and images, see my article on "The Place of Affect in Religious Education: Psychodynamics of Affectivity and Emotion," *Lumen Vitae* (Brussels), Vol. 26, No. 1, 1971, pp. 68-80; also the excellent work by James Hillman, *Emotion: A Comprehensive Phenomenology of Theories and Their Meanings for Therapy,* 2nd ed., Evanston, Illinois, Northwestern University Press, 1964.
5. See James L. Henderson, "Analytical Psychology and Education," *Lecture No. 87,* London, The Guild of Pastoral Psychology, 1973.
6. Paul Friedländer has described Plato's use of myth at length in Chapter IX of his *Plato: An Introduction,* 2nd ed., Princeton, New Jersey, Princeton University Press, 1969.

CHAPTER VII

1. See John Macquarrie, *Twentieth Century Religious Thought: The Frontiers of Philosophy and Theology, 1900-1960,* New York, Harper & Row, 1963, for a survey of this development.
2. Jerome D. Frank, M.D., *Persuasion and Healing: A Comparative Study of Psychotherapy,* New York, Schocken Books, 1969, p. 234.
3. See this book, C. G. Jung and C. Kerényi, *Essays on a Science of Mythology,* Princeton, New Jersey, Princeton University Press, 1969, particularly Jung's essay on "The Psychology of the Child Archetype," pp. 70-100, for an excellent understanding of the relation of myths to human development.
4. C. G. Jung, *Collected Works,* Vol. II *(Psychology and Religion: West and East)* , New York, Pantheon Books, 1958, p. 334.
5. See my God, *Dreams, and Revelation,* Minneapolis, Minnesota, Augsburg Publishing House, 1974, Chapter 8, for an account of this dream research.
6. C. G. Jung, *Collected Works,* Vol. 12 *(Psychology and Alchemy),* New York, Pantheon Books, 1953, p. 132.
7. C. G. Jung, *Collected Works,* Vol. 9, Part 2 *(Aion: Researches into the Phenomenology of the Self),* New York, Pantheon Books, 1959, pp. 33 f.
8. C. G. Jung, *Memories, Dreams, Reflections,* reccrded and edited by Aniela Jaffé, New York, Random House, 1963, pp. 351 f.

CHAPTER VIII

1. I have discussed the contributions of these men and several other important ones in the three studies I have written on religious experience—*Tongue Speaking* (which includes prophecy), *Healing and Christianity,* and *God, Dreams, and Revelation.*
2. This incident and the ultimate death of the child because of other factors is related by St. Gregory Nazianzen in his funeral oration "On St. Basil the Great." *Funeral Orations* by Saint Gregory Nazianzen and Saint Ambrose, New York, Fathers of the Church, Inc., 1953, pp. 71 f.
3. *Ibid.,* p. 322, (Saint Ambrose, "Funeral Oration on the Death of Emperor Theodosius."). Ambrose wrote about his dream in his letter to the emperor urging Theodosius to repent. In the dream, Ambrose wrote, "you appeared to have come to the church and I was not allowed to offer the Holy Sacrifice." Saint Ambrose, *Letters,* New York, Fathers of the Church, Inc., 1954, p. 24.
4. In a letter remaining from his later years, Aristotle wrote: "The more I find myself by myself and alone, the more I have become a lover of myth."

5. John Calvin, *Institutes of the Christian Religion,* I, ix, 6.
6. Joseph Campbell, *The Hero with a Thousand Faces,* New York, Meridian Books, 1956, p. 30.

CHAPTER X

1. This paper, "Transformation Symbolism in the Mass," is found in *Papers from the Eranos Yearbooks,* edited by Joseph Campbell, New York, Pantheon Books, Vol. 2, 1955, pp. 274-336; also in C. G. Jung, *Collected Works,* Vol. 11, *(Psychology and Religion: West and East),* New York, Pantheon Books, 1958, pp. 201-296.
2. Fr. Rahner's paper on "The Christian Mystery and the Pagan Mysteries" is found in *Papers from the Eranos Yearbooks,* Vol. 2, cited above, pp. 337-401.
3. For instance, there is a very interesting work, first published around the turn of the century, by Hugh W. White, a missionary to China, *Demonism Verified and Analyzed,* Ann Arbor, Michigan, University Microfilms, 1963; also the work by Fr. Leon Christiani, *Evidences of Satan in the Modern World,* New York, The Macmillan Co., 1962.